ARROYO CENTER

T0288861

The Value of Experience in the Enlisted Force

Jennie W. Wenger, Caolionn O'Connell, Louay Constant, Andrew J. Lohn

Prepared for the United States Army

Approved for public release; distribution unlimited

For more information on this publication, visit www.rand.org/t/RR2211

Library of Congress Cataloging-in-Publication Data is available for this publication.
ISBN: 978-1-9774-0040-6

Published by the RAND Corporation, Santa Monica, Calif.
© Copyright 2018 RAND Corporation
RAND® is a registered trademark.

*Cover: U.S. Army Forces Command's Command Sgt. Maj. Michael A. Grinston speaks
to Soldiers of E Company, 2nd Battalion, 506th Infantry Regiment, 3rd Brigade Combat Team,
101st Airborne Division at Ft. Campbell, 22 May, 2018. Photo by Sgt. Steven Lopez.*

Support RAND
Make a tax-deductible charitable contribution at
www.rand.org/giving/contribute

www.rand.org

Preface

This report documents research and analysis conducted as part of a project titled *The Value of Experience in the Enlisted Force*, cosponsored by the Assistant Secretary of the Army for Manpower and Reserve Affairs and by the Deputy Chief of Staff, G-1, U.S. Army. The purpose of the project was to provide information on the relationships among tenure, experience, and productivity within key noncommissioned officer leadership positions and to inform ongoing decisions about achieving reductions in Regular Army end strength that reduce personnel costs while maintaining or improving the quality of the noncommissioned officer corps.

The Project Unique Identification Code for the project that produced this document is HQD156887.

This research was conducted within RAND Arroyo Center's Personnel, Training, and Health Program. RAND Arroyo Center, part of the RAND Corporation, is a federally funded research and development center sponsored by the United States Army.

The RAND Corporation operates under a "Federal-Wide Assurance" (FWA00003425) and complies with the *Code of Federal Regulations for the Protection of Human Subjects Under United States Law* (45 CFR 46), also known as "the Common Rule," as well as with the implementation guidance set forth in U.S. Department of Defense (DoD) Instruction 3216.02. As applicable, this compliance includes reviews and approvals by RAND's Institutional Review Board (the Human Subjects Protection Committee) and by the U.S. Army. The views of sources utilized in this study are solely their own and do not represent the official policy or position of DoD or the U.S. Government.

Contents

Figures

Tables

Summary

Leading and mentoring soldiers is the primary mission of the U.S. Army's noncommissioned officers (NCOs). Per Army Doctrine Reference Publication 6-22, "confident, competent, and informed leadership intensifies the effectiveness of the other elements of combat power" (Headquarters, Department of the Army, 2012a, p. 1-1). Accordingly, the Army desires effective leaders and mentors because they motivate their soldiers to perform better. NCOs who do a better job at these tasks will be more likely to accomplish their mission *and* produce junior personnel who themselves go on to become strong leaders and mentors.

Given the central role of leadership and mentorship, it is somewhat surprising that past research has placed little emphasis on determining the relationship between NCOs and the performance of the junior soldiers under their command. However, given the complex nature of interactions among Army personnel and the frequent relocations that personnel undergo, relating a junior soldier's success to aspects of his or her leadership is difficult.

This study examined the influence of NCO leaders on their soldiers and whether the Army promotion process is capturing and retaining effective leaders. We linked junior and senior enlisted personnel and then tested the hypothesis that senior leaders' experience is related to the performance of junior personnel. We used three different variables to measure the performance of junior enlisted personnel: (1) attrition rates, (2) promotion rates, and (3) demotion rates. These three metrics were chosen to capture performance at various points along an enlisted soldier's career path. We tested several different measures of senior leaders' experience and included measures of leaders' other characteristics. The data used to conduct the analysis were drawn primarily from the Total Army Personnel Database.

As in other research, individual characteristics have a strong and significant relationship with early-term attrition, fast promotion, and likelihood of demotion. However, even when we corrected for individual characteristics of the junior soldiers, the characteristics and experience of senior leaders help predict differences in these junior soldier outcomes, and junior personnel have lower early-term attrition in cases in which senior leaders possess key types of experience. For example, attrition rates are higher among junior personnel under senior personnel who have less than 22 years of service.

However, more experience is not always a positive factor; rates are also slightly higher under senior personnel with more than 25 years of service. We find similar patterns with the number of months deployed; attrition rates are lowest when senior personnel have substantial deployment experience (20–39 months), but the attrition rate for junior personnel is higher when the senior leader has either less than 20 months *or* more than 39 months of deployment experience. This suggests that it is only certain types of leadership experience that improve the performance of junior soldiers. Furthermore, additional experience is not always preferable.

Having a leader with the right mix of experience can potentially generate substantial savings. To obtain a rough estimate of the potential savings, we compared the predicted attrition rates at two similar units that have different levels of senior leader experience. Our regression results indicate that a small unit with 100 junior soldiers would be expected to have an attrition rate between 12.4 percent and 14.4 percent, depending on the specific leadership characteristics. Thus, lowering attrition by 2 percentage points would mean that two additional soldiers would complete their initial terms of service, rather than leaving approximately two years prior to completing the term. Thus, senior leader experience can be expected to translate into about four additional years of service. This suggests that the Army would need to recruit about one fewer soldier for each unit with a leader of typical experience than for one with a less experienced leader.

Recruiting and training are expensive; recent estimates suggest that recruiting and training one soldier costs roughly $60,000. This suggests that having a more-experienced leader could translate into cost savings of as much as $60,000 even for a small unit. Of course, more-experienced leaders also require higher pay. Pay differences at the same rank but with different years of service are relatively modest, whereas pay grade differences are larger but still much less than the projected savings. These rough calculations suggest that the difference in cost between the least experienced leaders and leaders with desirable levels of experience is more than offset by the savings associated with lower levels of attrition. The $60,000 figure could be an under- or overestimate of the true cost, depending on what other changes within the Army structure are required to obtain leaders with desirable levels of experience at the unit level. Additionally, we acknowledge but do not examine the role of midgrade NCOs; to the extent that senior enlisted leaders with optimal levels of experience also assist in creating positive leadership skills among midgrade NCOs, our estimates may be conservative.

Given that experience matters in senior leaders and there is value to that experience, it is concerning that the Army promotion process captures only a limited amount of this experience since it solely considers deployment experience when promoting to E-5 and E-6. Additionally, Army doctrine and interviews with junior enlisted personnel identify multiple competencies and attributes associated with effective leadership, none of which is explicitly captured in the promotion process until promotion to E-7. These observations suggest that the Army may not be identifying soldiers with leadership potential early in their careers and fostering them accordingly. As a result, the Army may be losing effective leaders early and limiting the pool of senior NCOs. At this point, the mechanisms behind the relationship between experience and leadership skills are not yet clear, but there are a variety of ways in which the Army could account for time in service or grade in promotions to capture those benefits after gaining a better understanding of these mechanisms. For example, the Army may want to consider some elements of the NCO Evaluation Report earlier in the promotion pipeline to identify and encourage soldiers who demonstrate leadership potential. Potential quantitative approaches include considering promotion exams to identify knowledgeable soldiers and those proficient in their military occupational specialties.

Acknowledgments

We wish to express our gratitude to our sponsor and the staff in the Office of the Assistant Secretary of the Army for Manpower and Reserve Affairs, especially our action officer, Linden St. Clair, as well as the coordinators of our site visit. We would also like to thank the soldiers who took part in our interviews. At RAND, we thank Jan Hanley and Whitney Dudley for their work on building our analytical file. In addition, our colleagues Jim Crowley and Michael Shanley contributed timely analyses for subsections of this report; we are also indebted to Bryan Hallmark, Susan Straus, Chad Serena, and Andrea Golay for their contributions. We thank our summer associate, John Wittgenstein, for his many contributions to this research. We are grateful to our reviewers, Jim Hosek of RAND and Emerald Archer of Mount Saint Mary's University; their thoughtful comments and suggestions improved the quality of our work. Amy McGranahan, Cynthia Christopher, Martha Friese, and Mark Hvizda assisted in preparing the document.

Abbreviations

1SG	first sergeant
ADRP	Army Doctrine Reference Publication
AFQT	Armed Forces Qualification Test
ALC	Advanced Leader Course
ALRM	Army Leadership Requirements Model
ANCOC	Advanced Non-Commissioned Officer Course
APFT	Army physical fitness test
AR	Army Regulation
BNCOC	Basic Non-Commissioned Officer Course
CC	common core
CMF	career management fields
CSM	command sergeant major
DMDC	Defense Manpower Data Center
FA	field artillery
FY	fiscal year
GED	General Educational Development
HQDA	Headquarters, Department of the Army
MOS	military occupational specialty
MSG	master sergeant

MTOE	Modified Table of Organization and Equipment
NCO	noncommissioned officer
NCOER	Noncommissioned Officer Evaluation Report
NCOES	Noncommissioned Officer Education System
PLDC	Primary Leader Development Course
POI	program of instruction
SFC	sergeant first class
SLC	Senior Leader Course
SMC	Sergeants Major Course
SSD	Structured Self-Development
SSG	staff sergeant
TAPDB	Total Army Personnel Database
TDA	table of distribution and allowances
TIG	time in grade
TIS	time in service
UIC	unit identification code
VTT	video teletraining
WLC	Warrior Leader Course
YOS	year of service

CHAPTER ONE

Introduction

The Creed of the Noncommissioned Officer (NCO) states, in part,

> I am a Noncommissioned Officer, a leader of Soldiers. . . . My two basic responsibilities will always be uppermost in my mind—accomplishment of my mission and the welfare of my Soldiers. . . . I know my Soldiers and I will always place their needs above my own (Headquarters, Department of the Army [HQDA], 2015a).

Per Army Doctrine Reference Publication (ADRP) 6-22, "NCOs have roles as trainers, mentors, communicators, and advisors" (HQDA, 2012a). Additionally, the NCO Evaluation Report (NCOER) includes specific sections dedicated to leadership and training. Thus, leading and mentoring soldiers is the primary mission of the U.S. Army's NCOs. The strong implicit assumption is that leadership and mentorship matter: NCOs who do a better job at these tasks will be more likely to accomplish their missions *and* produce junior personnel who themselves go on to become strong leaders and mentors.

Given the central roles of leadership and mentorship, it is somewhat surprising that past research has placed little emphasis on determining the relationship between NCOs and the performance of the junior soldiers under their command. However, given the complex nature of interactions between Army personnel and the frequent relocations that personnel undergo, relating a junior soldier's success to aspects of his or her leadership is difficult.

This study examined the influence of NCO leaders on their soldiers and whether the Army promotion process is capturing and retaining effective leaders. We focus on the Regular Army.

Achieving Competence Through Experience

The commonly accepted method for achieving competence and capability as an NCO is through experience. Senior NCOs have a depth and breadth of experience that is likely to enable them to perform better on many tasks than more-junior personnel. In contrast, junior NCOs may provide innovative perspectives and approaches and may foster a different unit climate. It seems likely that experience, or tenure, raises productivity on many measures; thus, more-senior personnel are likely to be more valuable to the Army. However, more-senior personnel are also more costly.

Many studies in other fields have examined the correlations between leadership performance and various experience measures. Some of these studies show that inexperienced leaders performed better than experienced leaders under low-stress conditions, whereas experienced leaders performed better under stressful conditions. The proposed explanation for these results is that leaders under stress rely on their intuition; when based on a greater range of experience, this intuition and hence their performance is better. Under low-stress conditions, the more-experienced leaders are not as challenged and tend to cut corners and, as a result, underperform (Fiedler, 1996). We discuss the literature in more detail in Chapter Two.

Relevant Measures of Experience

The most straightforward measure of a soldier's experience is time spent in the Army (time in service [TIS]); a more detailed measure is time spent in a specific rank (time in grade). The Army measures a soldier's competence and capability in ways beyond tenure. In particular, Army education courses are designed to increase the competence of personnel; several courses play a key role in the development of NCOs. Also, in the current climate, many soldiers have accrued substantial levels of deployment experience. According to results published from the Annual Survey of Army Leadership conducted by the Center for Army Leadership, 83 percent of respondents reported that their deployment experience has had a large or positive impact on their development (Riley et al., 2014).

Description of Methodology

In this research, we linked junior and senior enlisted personnel based on their locations, then tested the hypothesis that senior leaders' experience is related to the performance of junior personnel. We tested several different measures of senior leaders' experience, as well as other characteristics of the leaders. We then present results for several different measures of junior soldiers' performance.

Our report is organized as follows: Chapter Two discusses some of the relevant literature on leadership and the implications for the Army. Chapter Three presents our empirical results on the relationship between senior leaders' experience and junior soldiers' performance. In Chapter Four, we examine the Army's promotion process in more detail and discuss the findings from our interviews with soldiers about positive and negative aspects of leadership. In Chapter Five, we examine promotion and retention speeds at key career milestones. Chapter Six discusses the implications of our findings. Appendixes contain additional empirical results, an examination of the NCO Education System, and the protocol used in our interviews.

CHAPTER TWO

The Literature Indicates Good Leaders Can Increase Effectiveness

This chapter summarizes the findings from prior research about the effect leadership has on direct or indirect followers. We describe some of the academic research that has quantified how various desirable leadership traits have affected followers. This includes education research, management literature, and analyses of military units. Additionally, we discuss Army doctrine as it pertains to the benefits of good leadership.

Academic Literature on Leadership

The topics of experience and leadership are quite broad in nature; potentially relevant literature can be found in many different areas. Examples include education literature on teacher experience and student outcomes and management literature on aspects of leadership that foster success and affect employee retention. The next section presents a summary of this literature.

Effective and Experienced Leaders Improve Overall Job Performance

Rich's (1997) findings indicate that salespeople had more loyalty to and trust in sales managers who were perceived to be role models. In turn, the more that salespeople have trust in or loyalty toward their sales managers, the greater the salespeople's overall job performance.

Some academic leadership models (e.g., Bass, 1991) differentiate between transactional and transformational leaders. *Transactional leaders* exert influence by setting goals, clarifying desired outcomes, providing feedback, and exchanging rewards for accomplishments. *Transformational leaders* exert additional influence by broadening and elevating the followers' goals and providing them with confidence to perform beyond the expectations specified in the implicit or explicit exchange agreement. These transformational leaders exhibit characteristics that arouse inspirational motivation, provide intellectual stimulation, and treat followers with individualized consideration.

Preferred models of leadership have been applied to other fields as well; for example, Dentsen (2003) found that, while some aspects of transitional leadership are related to reported effectiveness, time in current position is not relevant.[1] Koh, Steers, and Terborg (1995) found that transformational leadership in school principals had statistically significant positive effects on organizational citizenship, organizational commitment, and teacher satisfaction. In turn, these intermediate variables—citizenship, commitment, and satisfaction—had significant effects on the students' academic performance. Analysis of a longitudinal, randomized field experiment conducted with Israel Defence Forces found evidence that transformational leaders had a positive impact on even their indirect followers' performance, where performance was assessed by five routine Israel Defence Forces objective tests: written light weapon test, practical light weapon test, physical fitness test, obstacle course, and marksmanship. The written light weapon test, practical light weapon test, and obstacle course had statistically significant improvements under transformational leadership (Dvir et al., 2002).

Education-related research literature is also a rich source of data for examining experienced teachers, who can be considered leaders to their students. For example, Clotfelter, Ladd, and Vigno (2007) found clear evidence that teachers with more experience are more effective in raising student achievement than those with less experience. Those benefits appear to be linked to on-the-job experience rather than to graduate education, as having a graduate degree exerts no statistically significant positive effect on student achievement—in some cases, the effect is negative. Similarly, the work of Rivkin, Hanushek, and Kain (2005) supports the notion that mathematics teachers earlier in their careers perform significantly worse than more experienced teachers. It is worth noting that in the education literature, student characteristics generally dominate; while teachers affect student achievement, such factors as student poverty also have a large impact on achievement. For this reason, all of the studies cited here control for student background, and they all find that student background remains an important factor after controlling for school- and classroom-level characteristics.

Effective and Experienced Leaders Improve Retention

Effective leaders not only improve overall job performance, but they are also likely to improve employee retention. For example, Boyd et al. (2011) found that teachers' perceptions of a school administration's effectiveness and support had the greatest influence on a teacher's retention decisions. These results are not confined to education; Boyle et al. (1999) determined that nurse managers with a particular leadership style were more effective at retaining nurses. Managers with this leadership style sought out and valued contributions from the nursing staff, promoted information sharing, supported decisionmaking at the nursing staff level, exerted positional power, and influenced work coordination. Indeed, perceived supervisor support has been linked

---

[1] Dentsen's research used results of a survey of senior police officers in Australia to determined perceived effectiveness of those to whom they reported. We know of no studies in the law enforcement field that relate characteristics of senior leadership to performance or retention of junior personnel.

to reducing employee turnover in a variety of studies (Smith, 2005; Eisenberger et al., 2002; Maertz et al., 2007).

Literature on Army Leadership and Attrition

There is also a fairly substantial Army-specific literature on leadership and mentorship. ADRP 6-22 explains the Army's view of leadership and defines leadership as "the process of influencing people by providing purpose, direction, and motivation to accomplish the mission and improve the organization" (HQDA, 2012a). Per the Army, "confident, competent, and informed leadership intensifies the effectiveness of the other elements of combat power" (HQDA, 2012a). Accordingly, the Army desires effective leaders and mentors because they motivate their soldiers to perform better.

In the Army, there are several ways in which a good leader can increase organizational effectiveness. Effective NCO leaders focus on building a cohesive unit because "[i]t is proven that a team is more effective than an individual when members work together, using their unique skills, experiences, and capabilities" (HQDA, 2012a). According to leader development surveys (Riley et al., 2016), leaders reported that their own leadership skills had been developed most effectively through the direct experience of leading a unit, as well as on-the-job training, mentoring, and learning from peers.

There is a substantial body of research examining the success of military personnel. Much of this research focuses on enlisted personnel during the first term of service. Although some research focuses on other outcomes, in many cases, *success* is defined as completion of the initial term of service. Given the substantial costs associated with recruiting and training, this focus is not surprising. Several characteristics have been found to be strongly associated with first-term performance. First among those is education credential; enlistees with high school diplomas complete the first term at a higher rate than enlistees who lack this credential, a result that holds across services and time (see, e.g., Laurence, Naughton, and Harris, 1996, as well as Buddin, 2005). The reasons behind this relationship are not completely clear, but differences in noncognitive skills (such as motivation or interpersonal skills) provide a potential explanation (Wenger and Hodari, 2004). Other factors also help to explain retention rates; differences are correlated with gender, ethnicity (in some cases), and the existence of waivers (Buddin, 2005). Armed Forces Qualification Test (AFQT) scores are weakly associated with retention, but they also have some relationship with success in training (Laurence, Naughton, and Harris, 1996; Buddin, 2005).

It is worth noting that most research examining the behavior of enlisted personnel focuses on the first term and often on only the first 36 months. This constitutes a limited definition of success; it could even be thought of as a minimal definition. And although the results of this research suggest that education credentials and other characteristics mentioned here have significantly and substantively strong relationships with first-term performance, large performance differences exist within groups of "high-quality" soldiers and within groups of soldiers not classified as high quality. Indeed, many "high-quality" soldiers fail to complete the first term of service, and many other soldiers complete successful careers.

There is some research examining other outcomes. For example, there is evidence that aspects of service (as opposed to personal characteristics) influence completion and retention (see, for example, Hosek and Martorell, 2009, in which the authors report finding a relationship between deployments and retention). Finally, there is a limited amount of research examining other measures of success. Most relevant for this research is a group of reports that develop quality measures among enlisted personnel (Ward and Tan, 1985; Hosek and Mattock, 2003; Asch, Romley, and Totten, 2005). These reports use cross-service data on enlisted personnel from an earlier era (mid-1970s through the early 1990s) and develop a quality index or measure based, in part, on speed of promotion early in the career. The authors of these reports consistently found that the services retain fast promoters and thus retain higher-quality members than is revealed by tracking measures, such as AFQT scores or education credentials of those who remain. In each case, promotion speed is a driver in the quality index, generally offering more explanatory power than AFQT or education. Hosek and Mattock (2003) found that service members with higher measures on the quality index are more likely to reenlist; Asch, Romley, and Totten (2005) examined longer-term performance measures and found that those who are promoted to higher grades are of substantially higher quality than other enlistees. Essentially, this body of research indicates that the services' promotion processes are effective at rewarding and thus helping to retain the most effective personnel; however, the reports do not include any aspects of leadership. Lyle and Smith (2014) found that junior Army officers are promoted more quickly when they are assigned to mentors who themselves have histories of early promotion.

Conclusions

Prior academic research indicates that a skilled leader can increase followers' performance and encourage retention in a variety of sectors. Army doctrine accepts the results of this research and assumes that good leadership intensifies the effectiveness and cohesion of combat units. Using Army personnel data, we attempted to validate these academic results. In the next chapter, we discuss our data and how we measured the performance of junior enlisted personnel throughout their careers. We then estimate the extent to which the individual characteristics of a soldier, Army institutional factors, and senior enlisted leadership affect junior enlisted soldiers' performance.

CHAPTER THREE

Leader Experience and Soldier Performance

Given the extensive research that indicates that effective leadership is likely to improve overall job performance and follower retention, whether indirectly or directly, we develop measures of leadership and test the relationship using a data set of Army enlisted personnel.

The data used to conduct the analysis were drawn primarily from the Total Army Personnel Database (TAPDB),[1] which includes a wide variety of information on enlisted personnel throughout their careers; pertinent examples include basic demographic information (gender, race, age at enlistment), highest degree attained at enlistment, and AFQT score. Also captured in the TAPDB is information on the fiscal year (FY) of enlistment, promotion dates, demotion dates (if any), and reason for separation for those who leave the Army. Finally, the TAPDB includes a unit identification code (UIC) that indicates unit assignment on a monthly basis.

We formed our basic sample of junior soldiers by selecting soldiers who entered the Regular Army in FYs 2002–2014. Of this initial sample, we then selected only the soldiers who completed initial training and were assigned to combat-ready, deployable (Modified Table of Organization and Equipment [MTOE]) units within 15 months of entering the Army.[2] We selected MTOE units because their structure offers a fairly straightforward method of identifying senior enlisted leaders of these units.[3] This group includes roughly one-half of all soldiers who entered the Army

---

[1] We derived information on deployment experience from a Defense Manpower Data Center (DMDC) database, the Contingency Tracking System Deployment File.

[2] MTOE units are combat ready and deploy; in contrast, table of distribution and allowances (TDA) units are not combat ready and do not deploy. Some examples of TDA units include schoolhouses, base hospitals, and HQDA; such units can have a more inflated rank structure with fewer junior officers and enlisted soldiers than MTOE units. Given that this analysis focuses on capturing the influence of senior NCO leadership on their subordinate soldiers, we felt that many of those units would not help us capture those effects; therefore, we excluded TDA units from our analyses. Thus, soldiers in the combat arms–type professions are somewhat overrepresented in our sample.

[3] These MTOE units have a traditional unit hierarchy in that the first four characters of the UIC identify the battalion. From this, we could identify the highest-ranked enlisted soldier.

during our sample period and more than one-half of all soldiers who entered combat arms career management fields (CMFs).

Key NCO leadership roles are defined in Army Regulation (AR) 600-20, "Army Command Policy" (HQDA, 2014). They include the following:

- *Sergeant major of the Army.* This is the senior sergeant major grade and designates the senior enlisted position of the Army. The sergeant major in this position serves as the senior enlisted adviser and consultant to the Chief of Staff of the Army.
- *Command sergeant major (CSM).* This position title designates the senior NCO of the command at battalion or higher levels. It carries out policies and standards and advises the commander on the performance, training, appearance, and conduct of enlisted soldiers. The CSM administers the unit NCO's development program.
- *First sergeant (1SG).* The position of 1SG designates the senior NCO at company level. The 1SG of a separate company- or equivalent-level organization administers the unit NCO's professional development program.
- *Platoon sergeant.* The platoon sergeant is the key assistant and adviser to the platoon leader. In the absence of the platoon leader, the platoon sergeant leads the platoon.
- *Section, squad, and team leaders.* These direct leaders are the NCOs responsible at this level.

Matching junior soldiers to their senior NCO leaders was a key aspect of our estimation strategy. We matched personnel as follows: We used the fifth digit of the UIC to determine the company; we then identified the highest-ranking soldier in the headquarters company by pay grade and job title.[4] We then developed several measures of experience and calculated the experience level on each measure for the senior NCO. Our measures of experience include TIS, TIG, time in unit, and deployment experience (each was measured at the time the junior and senior soldiers were matched and serving in the same unit). We also included an indicator that the senior soldier was promoted more quickly than average to E-6.[5] Our senior leaders were mostly E-9s, but about 28 percent were E-8s. These senior NCOs were likely in CSM or 1SG leadership positions. These soldiers typically had spent more than 24 years in the Army, although about one-quarter had spent less than 22 years and another one-quarter had spent at

---

[4] Two members of our study team with relevant experience sorted through job titles to determine the most senior NCOs; we compared the decisions made by the two team members and found a very high level of agreement, suggesting that we had successfully identified the senior NCO in each unit. When senior personnel of equal job titles and experience overlapped, we formed a measure based on the average of their experience levels.

[5] We experimented with several measures of promotion speed to E-6. We present measures based on relative promotion speed (speed compared with that of other soldiers in the same cohort and CMF). The results are similar when we used an absolute standard—promotion to E-6 by 64 months.

least 26.8 years. A typical senior leader had spent just more than 24 months in the current unit.[6] (See Table A.1 in Appendix A for more descriptive information on senior leaders.)

We measured several characteristics of senior leaders (TIS, time deployed, time in current unit); the extent to which these characteristics are correlated provides helpful information about how to interpret our results (see Table A.2 in Appendix A). As expected, time in the Army and time deployed are positively correlated; months to E-6 is also positively correlated with both of these measures. This could indicate that deployments defer promotion or could be driven by the fact that promotion speeds and deployment probabilities vary over the period included in our sample. AFQT, generally considered a measure of quality, is negatively correlated with time to E-6 and with time in the Army; this is consistent with faster promotions for higher-quality soldiers (although the distribution of AFQT scores has also varied over time). Time in the current MTOE unit is higher among those who have spent more time deployed, but it is not correlated with months to E-6. Furthermore, the correlation between months in the unit and AFQT scores is positive but weak (significant only at the 10-percent level, suggesting that the relationship could occur by chance). Taken together, these measures suggest that those with the highest levels of deployment experience would be expected to have relatively high AFQT scores and levels of Army experience, but these leaders would not necessarily have been the fastest promoted to E-6. In contrast, fast promoters (based on E-6 promotion) would be expected to have less time in the Army than others and slightly lower AFQT scores. It is possible that the fastest promoters are of somewhat lower quality than other senior enlisted leaders; we discuss this point in more detail in Chapter Three. In short, it is not clear that all high-quality markers tend to be correlated; rather, it appears that senior enlisted personnel have various combinations of attributes. Mostly, these attributes are not correlated with time at current unit, suggesting that time in unit is determined by other factors.

The TAPDB is a monthly file, and we matched junior soldiers in our data set to the senior-most enlisted soldier in their units each month; leader experience is determined by the characteristics of the leader in the current month.[7] Thus, leaders who remain in units become more experienced, and our measure of leader experience reflects this as months pass. Junior soldiers in our data set spend, on average, nearly two years in the first MTOE unit; a typical senior leader spends more than two years in the unit. Thus, while turnovers are not rare, junior personnel appear to have significant exposure to many of their senior leaders.

---

[6]   We have observations over multiple months on nearly every senior leader in our data set; the statistics in this paragraph are calculated based on the last observation we have for each senior leader. Thus, the leaders were somewhat less experienced during the first month in each unit.

[7]   Occasionally, personnel overlap (e.g., a new leader may arrive before the previous leader departs). In those cases, we determined the experience level as an average of the experience of the two enlisted leaders.

Performance Indicators

Our analysis used three different variables to measure the performance of junior enlisted personnel: (1) attrition rates, (2) promotion rates, and (3) demotion rates. These three metrics were chosen to capture performance at various points along an enlisted soldier's career path. As shown in Figure 3.1, the attrition rate captures whether an enlisted soldier adapts to the Army's culture within the first 36 months of service. A soldier's promotion speed to E-5, which on average occurs about 45 months from enlistment, can serve as a proxy for overall soldier performance. Finally, the probability of demotion within 24 months of attaining the rank of E-5 captures whether a soldier's performance falls short of Army standards.

The Army cares about soldier attrition rates as it does employee retention rates. Here, we calculated our attrition rate as the percentage of soldiers who separated because of "failure to adapt"—reflecting a loss of investment to the Army and a likely indicator of poor performance. It is important to note that we formed our sample based on soldiers who completed initial training and were assigned to MTOE units. Therefore, the substantial amount of first-term attrition that occurs within the first year is *not* reflected in our attrition numbers, and our attrition rates are substantially lower than those reported for overall first-term attrition. Our sample was based on completion of initial training, however, an additional 12–15 percent of soldiers leave the Army prior to completing 36 months of service for failure-to-adapt reasons.

Prior RAND research (Hosek and Mattock, 2003, among others) has argued that speed of promotion can serve as a measure of performance. While early-term promotions are generally automatic and occur on a highly predictable timetable, many factors are considered when promoting a soldier to E-5 and above (see Chapter Four for more information about the promotion process). These factors include military training, military education, civilian education, awards, decorations and achievements—all

Figure 3.1
Performance Metrics Along the Army Enlisted Career Path by Months of Service

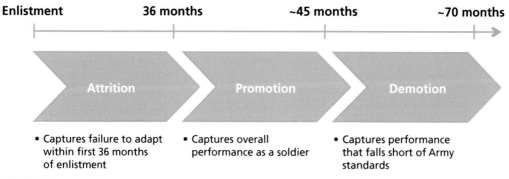

of which are useful indicators of quality. As a result, our analysis assumed that junior enlisted soldiers who attain the rank of E-5 faster than their peers were considered better soldiers by the Army at the time they were promoted.

Demotions are relatively rare, but the vast majority of demotions occur at a specific point in a soldier's career—after being promoted to E-5. Indeed, most demotions occur within 24 months of promotion to E-5. Demotions can occur for a variety of reasons, from misconduct to "inefficiency"—defined as a soldier's inability to perform duties and responsibilities commensurate with his or her current rank and military occupational specialty (MOS). Regardless of the cause, demotions are considered unfavorable and an indication of performance that falls short of Army standards. To create a measure that is more comparable across soldiers, we limited our demotion analysis to the 24 months following promotion to E-5.

Technical Description of Indicators

We posited that there are multiple factors that influence soldier performance; consequently, we modeled our performance indicators as a function of individual, institutional, and leadership factors. More detail on our empirical model is provided in Appendix A.

Attrition Rates

The attrition rate analysis used separation codes that are assigned to soldiers leaving the Army, and we grouped reasons for separation into one of four broad categories: (1) failure to adapt; (2) completed term; (3) promoted or moved to officer or reserve status; or (4) missing in action, killed in action, or disabled. We considered only failure-to-adapt attrition here; thus, our attrition rate was calculated as the proportion of soldiers who left the Army prior to 36 months for a reason in the failure-to-adapt category.[8] There are more than 100 different designations for separations; failure-to-adapt attrition includes separations that could be classified as occurring because the soldier struggled to adapt to the Army system. A few examples include discharge because of misconduct, weight control failure, and desertion. Figure 3.2 shows failure-to-adapt 24- and 36-month attrition rates for the years included in our sample.

Our definition of attrition for reasons related to adaptability is an attempt to capture attrition decisions that are closely related to junior soldiers' behaviors and decisions and thus are most likely to be affected by leadership. However, we also analyzed 48-month continuation rates as a specification check; the continuation results were consistent with the 36-month attrition results and therefore are not included in the

---

[8]   By the time they have been in the Army for 36 months, all soldiers who do not leave the Army for failure-to-adapt reasons either remain in the Army or fall into one of the other three stated categories.

Figure 3.2
Attrition Rates by Fiscal Year of Enlistment, Conditional on Completion of Initial Training and Reaching First Modified Table of Organization and Equipment Unit

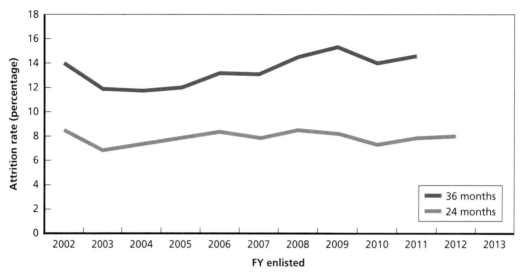

SOURCES: TAPDB and DMDC data.
RAND *RR2211-3.2*

main body of this report.[9] Again, our attrition rates reported here are conditional on soldiers completing initial training and being assigned to MTOE battalions.

Promotion Speed

We considered several measures of promotion speed, eventually settling on a measure that indicates promotion to E-5 within 36 months of entering the Army. Roughly 30 percent of those promoted to E-5 are promoted to E-5 within 36 months of entering the Army. Although overall promotion rates to E-5 within 36 months vary somewhat over the period included in our sample, our results were similar to alternative measures that attempted to allow for differences in promotion rates over time and across MOSs.

Demotion Rate

Demotions are rare across our entire sample; less than 2 percent of the junior soldiers in our sample experienced a demotion. But many soldiers left the Army prior to the point at which most demotions occur. Most demotions occur at E-5; of only soldiers who were promoted to E-5, about 6 percent were demoted. Most often, the demotion was to E-4, although some demotions were to lower pay grades. We further focused on demotions that occur within 24 months of promotion to E-5; this cutoff was selected

---

[9]   See Appendix A for more information.

Figure 3.3
Pattern of Demotions After Promotion to E-5

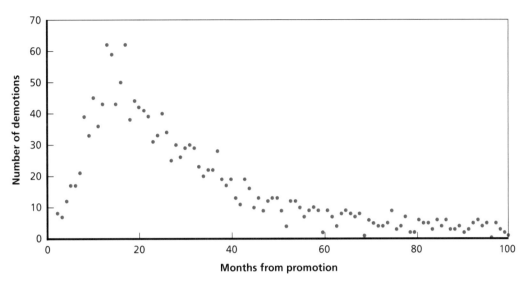

SOURCES: TAPDB and DMDC data.
RAND RR2211-3.3

because the majority of E-5 demotions happen within the first two years and because it allows analysis of cohorts as recent as FY 2012.

Figure 3.3 illustrates the number of demotions as a function of months from promotion to E-5; the data include soldiers who completed initial training and were assigned to MTOE units within 15 months of entering the Army. Approximately 2,400 demotions from E-5 occurred in our data set; about two-thirds of these occurred within 24 months of E-5 promotion. We considered only demotions that lasted for at least three months (in some cases, pay grade decreases during one month and then increases in the following month; such instances may represent errors in the administrative file). Across our sample, about 4 percent of E-5s had demotions within 24 months of being promoted that lasted at least three months; the rate of demotions was relatively constant across the time period included in our data.

Next, we present our empirical results based on the sample that includes junior enlisted personnel who entered the Army in FYs 2002–2014, measures of their individual characteristics, institutional factors, and the levels of experience of their leaders.

Results: Attrition

Throughout the results sections, the blue horizontal lines on the figures mark the baseline probability of the outcome (attrition, demotion, promotion).[10] The vertical blue bars represent the 95-percent confidence intervals for the probability of the outcome when the baseline demographic for that category is replaced with the corresponding value labeled on the horizontal axis. Estimates that are statistically significant have blue bars that do not overlap the baseline (statistical significance reflects a low probability that the relationship occurred by chance, less than a 5-percent probability in the case of these estimates, although many of the estimates presented here would be predicted to occur by chance far less than one in 100 times).

Senior leader characteristics are associated with attrition, even if we hold constant all of the other factors in our model (see Figure 3.4). Specifically, attrition rates are higher among junior personnel when senior personnel have less than 22 years of service (YOSs). However, more experience is not always a positive factor; rates are also

Figure 3.4
Probability of 36-Month Attrition as a Function of Senior Leader Characteristics

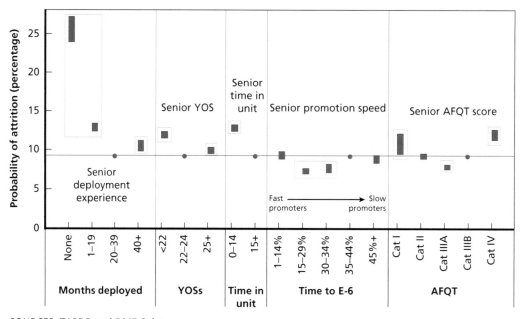

SOURCES: TAPDB and DMDC data.
NOTES: Blue horizontal line is the baseline probability of the outcome (attrition, demotion, promotion). The AFQT is scored on a percentile system; the categories are defined as follows: cat I: score of 93–99; cat II: score of 65–92; cat IIIA: score of 50–64; cat IIIB: score of 31–49; and cat IV: score of 30 or lower.
RAND RR2211-3.4

---

[10] The baseline probability was calculated for a white male with a high school diploma and an AFQT score in the category (cat) IIIB who enlisted at age 19.

slightly higher when senior personnel have at least 25 YOSs. We find similar patterns with senior enlisted personnel's months deployed; attrition rates are lowest when senior personnel have substantial deployment experience (20–39 months of deployment experience), and the attrition rate of junior personnel increases when those senior personnel have what can be considered too little or too much deployment experience.[11] Senior time to E-6 demonstrates a similar pattern: Junior personnel have lower rates of attrition when senior personnel were neither the fastest nor the slowest in terms of promotion to E-6.

Our results are consistent across our measures of senior leader experience: In each case, junior personnel have higher attrition under senior personnel with low levels of experience. But higher levels of experience are not always associated with lower levels of junior personnel attrition. Junior attrition is higher in units with the most-experienced leaders than in those with moderately experienced leaders.

There are many ways to measure and model experience; we included only a few measures, and we modeled experience using categorical variables, both for ease of interpretation and to allow for nonlinear results. Our strategy in forming these variables was to draw the lines between categories to separate out the top and bottom quartiles of the distribution. For example, about 25 percent of the junior personnel in our sample had senior leaders with less than 22 YOSs; about 25 percent had senior leaders with at least 25 YOSs, and about 50 percent had leaders with 22–24 YOSs. In the case of senior deployment experience, we created a category to indicate that a leader had no deployment experience; although this group is small, we posited that results could be different for those whose leaders had no deployment experience. Nearly one-quarter of the sample had senior leaders with one to 19 months of deployment experience, nearly one-quarter had senior leaders with at least 40 months experience, and the rest had senior leaders with 20–39 months of deployment experience.[12] We calculated senior promotion speed based on the time to E-6 relative to others in the same cohort; the fastest promoters (1–14 percent) were promoted faster than at least 86 percent of their cohort, but, by the time they reached senior leadership positions, nearly one-fifth of

[11] Attrition rates are substantially higher in units in which senior personnel have no deployment experience than in those in which senior personnel have some experience. However, we note that this represents a very small group of leaders (less than 3 percent of all leaders), and most were observed only during the earliest years included in our data set (prior to 2006). Some of these soldiers may have experienced injuries prior to assuming their leadership positions; some may have changed MOSs during their careers or served in MOSs in which deployment is less common.

[12] In Table A.1 in Appendix A, we provide descriptive statistics on these variables. However, note that Table A.1 provides measures based on the sample of *leaders*, not the sample of junior soldiers. For example, Table A.1 indicates that about 17 percent of leaders have less than 22 YOSs, while 39 percent have at least 25 YOSs. This suggests that those who are promoted quickly tend to serve as leaders to more junior soldiers than those promoted more slowly.

junior soldiers had leaders who were promoted this quickly.[13] In contrast, the senior AFQT score groups are not the same size; few leaders have cat I scores.[14]

The amount of time that the senior enlisted leader has spent in the unit is also tied to attrition when controlling for the other measures in the model; attrition rates are higher for junior soldiers whose senior enlisted leaders have spent less than 15 months in their (initial) MTOE units, and the effect is roughly the same size as the expected difference between a leader with 20 years of experience and one with 23 years of experience. Thus, unit-specific experience appears to matter. This result suggests that transitions between leaders can be costly. Given the fact that *all* senior enlisted leaders (regardless of level of experience) transition into new units, there may be ways to mitigate this effect; we discuss this in more detail in a later section.

All NCOs complete a series of Army education courses designed to prepare them for their roles as leaders. We explored the effects of these courses in several different ways. First, we included course completion as a senior trait. However, virtually all senior personnel completed these (required) courses, and there was not enough variation for us to identify a relationship between completion and junior soldier attrition. Next, we tested the hypothesis that junior personnel would perform differently if their leadership completed the courses shortly before the junior soldiers' arrival at the unit. We found little evidence of this. Finally, we explored the changes in NCO education courses over time. However, only a few leaders in our data set completed the courses after the changes were in place; consequently, we were unable to discern any relationship. Therefore, we analyzed the content of the courses to determine how the changes in the courses will likely impact current and future soldiers. Our results, included in Appendix B, suggest that the updated NCO education courses likely place less emphasis on key aspects of leadership than past courses do, but our analyses also suggest that the changes would be expected to have little impact on the productivity measures we examine here (see Appendix B for the details of our analysis of course content). In summary, it seems unlikely that the current coursework will produce future leaders who are better prepared for the leadership aspects of their jobs than today's senior personnel.

Our models also include soldiers' individual characteristics, as well as an indicator of the base location. Some of these variables have strong and significant relationships with early-term attrition for failure-to-adapt reasons, even in our regression model that holds many other factors constant. Despite limiting our sample to soldiers at their first MTOE unit, many our findings are consistent with those of other researchers.[15] For

---

[13] We present results in this manner to be consistent with our results in Chapter Five; dividing the seniors into fewer "time to E-6" groups produces similar results.

[14] A cat I score is a score at the 93rd percentile or higher.

[15] We estimated parallel models explaining 48-month failure-to-adapt attrition and explaining 36- and 48-month continuation. The results are broadly similar with those presented here. This is not surprising in the case of 48-month attrition, as most failure-to-adapt attrition occurs within the first 36 months. The differences can be explained by the fact that continuations do not include those who are injured or killed, those who have

example, women have higher attrition rates than men, and education levels are highly correlated with attrition; those who lack high school diplomas leave the Army at higher rates than soldiers who enlist after completing high school. These results appear in Figures A.1 and A.2 in Appendix A.[16]

To summarize, some of the characteristics of the senior leader in the unit are strongly associated with early-term failure-to-adapt attrition. Next, we present parallel analyses of other measures of junior soldier success: rates of promotion and rates of demotion.

Results: Promotion

As discussed, we focused on a single measure of promotion speed: promotion to E-5 within 36 months of entering the Army. We find that some characteristics of senior enlisted leaders are related to the promotion speed of junior personnel, although most are unrelated (and thus many of the blue bars in Figure 3.5 overlap the horizontal line). Junior enlisted personnel are less likely to be promoted quickly to E-5 when the senior enlisted leader has more deployment experience. While we do not know the exact mechanism behind this finding, it is possible that senior leaders with more deployment experience apply promotion criteria in a stricter manner or in a manner that rewards somewhat different traits. Promotion rates are also slightly slower when senior personnel have AFQT scores in the range of 50–64 and when the senior personnel themselves promoted slowly to E-6. While the mechanism behind this final finding is not immediately clear, we note that it is consistent with the research on officer promotions by Lyle and Smith (2014).

As was the case for attrition, we included measures of the junior soldiers' characteristics and the base locations. These results indicate that there are few differences in promotion rates across bases but that junior soldiers' characteristics are strongly related to promotion (see Figures A.3 and A.4 in Appendix A).

Results: Demotion

In general, characteristics of the leader at the soldier's first unit are not associated with demotions in a statistically significant manner (see Figure 3.6). This is not especially

---

become officers, or those who have completed their terms of service (unlikely by 36 months, but more common by 48 months). These results can be found in Appendix A. For an example of other work in the area, see Buddin (2005).

[16] Complete regression results can be found in Appendix A. Note that the regression results for all figures in this chapter hold constant the other characteristics (e.g., individual, institutional, or senior) not illustrated, as well as FY and quarter of enlistment.

Figure 3.5
Probability of Early Promotion to E-5 as a Function of Leader Characteristics

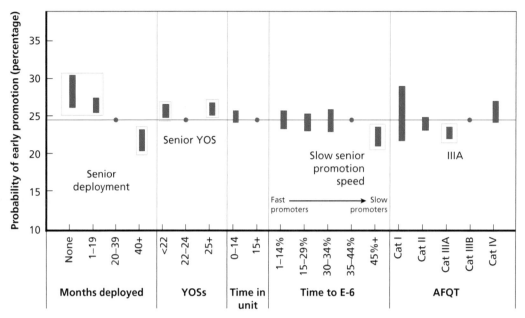

SOURCES: TAPDB and DMDC data.
NOTE: Blue horizontal line is the baseline probability of the outcome (attrition, demotion, promotion).
RAND RR2211-3.5

surprising for at least two reasons. First, in many cases, the soldier is no longer at the initial unit during the 24 months following promotion to E-5; therefore, the characteristics of the first leader would be expected to be less relevant for this outcome than for early-term attrition, although it is certainly possible that early leaders influence later outcomes, such as demotions. Second, demotion is, in some ways, a different type of outcome from attrition; while both certainly reflect decisions and behavior of the junior soldier, demotions might be expected to hew closely to well-defined Army policies regarding misconduct, per ARs 600-8-19 and 27-10 (HQDA, 2017; HQDA, 1996). Therefore, we might expect senior leader characteristics (as well as the location of the installation) to be less relevant. Additionally, demotion might be the most likely of the outcomes we considered to occur due to impulsive actions (while promotion and even attrition may occur due to actions that happen over a longer period of time). If this is the case, we might expect leadership to have less influence over impulsive actions and behaviors than over actions and behaviors that occur over a course of weeks or months. Finally, it is possible that demotion-related decisions are made not at the unit level but at a lower level in the Army's organizational structure (below the headquarters company), and perhaps NCOs who are subordinate to the senior leader are more

Figure 3.6
Probability of Demotion from E-5 as a Function of Leader Characteristics

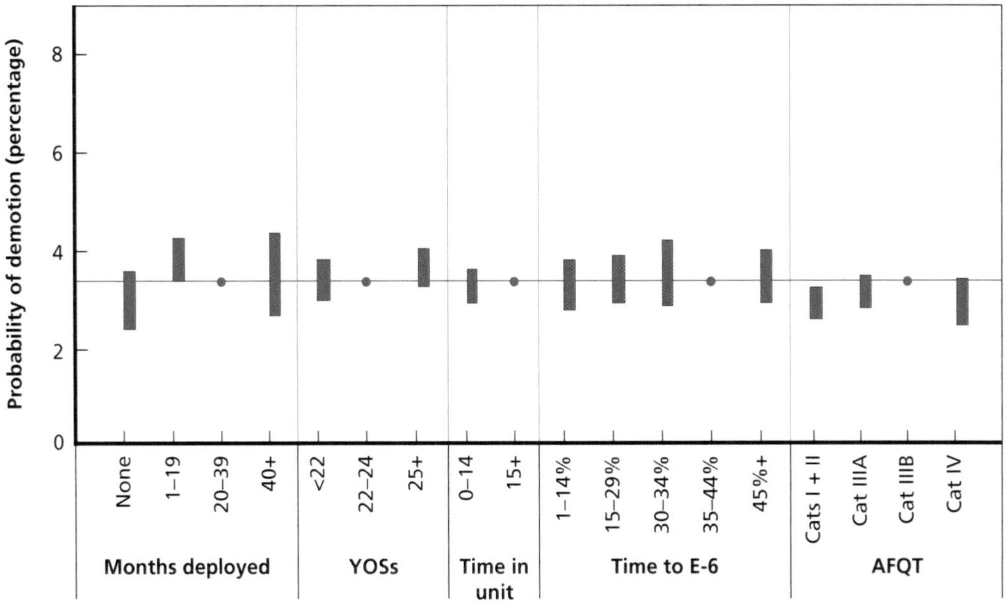

SOURCES: TAPDB and DMDC data.
NOTE: Blue horizontal line is the baseline probability of the outcome (attrition, demotion, promotion).
RAND RR2211-3.6

involved in such policies. This suggests that the specific way in which this analysis identified the relationship between junior and senior soldiers have limited our findings.

As was the case for attrition and promotion, the soldiers' own characteristics are strongly correlated with the likelihood of demotion; in the case of demotions, there are only minimal differences across bases (see Figures A.5 and A.6 in Appendix A).

Defining Junior–Senior Army Personnel Relationships

In these results, we define the junior–senior relationship based on the UIC, company, and job title. While this methodology is intuitively appealing and offers the possibility of precisely identifying the unit leader, it may miss some important aspects of mentorship or leadership. In particular, mentorship and leadership surely occur at lower levels within the unit.[17] Therefore, we also tested several other methods of identifying the senior enlisted leader for each junior enlisted soldier. As with the estimates just pre-

---

[17] Indeed, midgrade NCOs also play an important leadership role within units; we were not able to explicitly capture that relationship in this effort, but we discuss some implications and potential extensions in the final chapter of the report.

sented, we continued to define the relationship by the unit, seeking out soldiers who served at the same unit at the same time. The UIC is a six-character description of each unit: The first four characters describe the unit, the fifth character refers to the company (headquarters, A company, B company), and the sixth character discerns organic units, which may, in some cases, be assigned to different commands. Thus, each additional character identifies a smaller group of people.

We tested alternative specifications in which we defined the leader–follower relationship by simply identifying as the leader the soldier with the highest pay grade at each (four-, five-, or six-character) UIC. Our results are broadly similar under these alternative strategies of identifying the leader of each unit: Individual characteristics remain important, but leadership characteristics also affect some outcomes. As was the case in Figures 3.4–3.6, leadership characteristics are less likely to be statistically significant in models explaining demotion and early promotion versus attrition. One interpretation of this is that Army leadership across a unit is fairly consistent: The CSM's influence extends to those who are identified as leaders at the smaller unit (five- or six-digit UIC) level.[18]

However, there are a few differences when we identify leaders using this alternative methodology. For example, when we identify the leader by using the six-digit UIC, we identify some leaders who are E-7s (all of our leadership in the other strategies are E-8s or E-9s). In the case of E-7s and demotion, demotion rates are measurably higher at the relatively small number of six-digit units with E-7s serving as senior leaders.[19] Recall that this result holds years of service constant. One interpretation of this is that soldiers who are promoted to E-8 or E-9 create an atmosphere in which demotion is less likely to occur. Despite these differences, these results suggest that it is possible to discern leadership effects in a fairly straightforward manner simply by selecting the senior person with the highest level of experience within each unit.

In conclusion, our results consistently suggest that experience is valuable; key aspects of leaders' experience are associated with lower levels of attrition among junior soldiers. However, more experience is not always preferable.

---

[18] We might expect that we would be less likely to discern relationships at the five- or six-digit UIC level simply because the sample sizes are smaller. However, recall that our sample is a soldier-unit sample with measures of leader experience; the sample thus is fairly large and even at the six-digit level, we typically have several hundred observations of each unit. While sample size surely would become important at a more disaggregated level, the fact that our results are similar if we define units by four-, fix-, or six-digit UIC code suggests that sample sizes are not limiting our analyses.

[19] Even using the six-digit code for identification, fewer than 10 percent of units were led by an E-7.

CHAPTER FOUR

Does the Army Capture Good Leaders in the Promotion Process?

Given that some deployment experience and longer TIG and TIS for senior enlisted personnel are correlated with lower attrition of subordinates, the data indicate that experience matters for senior leaders. These results invite the question whether the Army is giving sufficient credit for that experience in the promotion process.

Many factors are considered when promoting a soldier to E-5 and above. These factors include military training, military education, civilian education, awards, decorations, and achievements—all of which are arguably useful indicators of quality. Unfortunately, the Army's promotion process does not include many other indicators that might help identify promising leaders until a soldier reaches E-7. This chapter discusses the Army's promotion process and makes recommendations for improving that process to capture leadership *potential* earlier in a soldier's career.

Army Doctrine Defines Leadership Requirements

In addition to explaining the Army's view on leadership, ADRP 6-22 describes the desirable attributes and core leader competencies associated with these leaders (HQDA, 2012a). The Army captures these attributes and competencies in the Army Leadership Requirements Model (ALRM). Figure 4.1 illustrates the fundamental components of the ALRM.

Attributes refers to the innate characteristics that make for an effective leader. *Competencies* refers to the skills and learnable behavior that the Army expects leaders to acquire. In effect, attributes are enablers for competencies.

In addition to ARDP 6-22, the Army's Field Manual 6-22 "provides a doctrinal framework covering methods for leaders to develop other leaders, improve their organizations, build teams, and develop themselves" (HQDA, 2015b). For example, Field Manual 6-22 links leadership requirements to the principles of mission command, discusses available leadership development programs, and guides soldiers through the fundamentals of leadership and how they might further develop those skills.

Figure 4.1
The Army Leadership Requirements Model

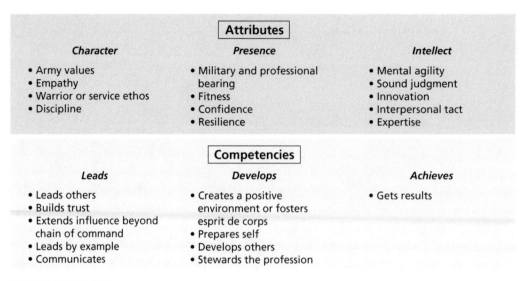

SOURCE: HQDA, 2012a.
RAND RR2211-4.1

Qualitative Interviews with Soldiers Were Aligned with Doctrine

Although Army doctrine defines NCO leadership attributes and core competencies, it is important to ensure that doctrine aligns with soldiers' values and experiences. To that end, we interviewed soldiers to understand the qualities they attributed to effective Army leadership based on their personal experiences. We then compared soldiers' responses with Army doctrine to determine whether there was alignment between the two.

We used semistructured interviews to collect qualitative data on soldiers' experience with Army leadership. We interviewed 19 soldiers from a variety of ranks, CMFs, and units. The personnel interviewed varied in rank from E-2 through E-5, with a commensurate TIS variation from one to 13 years. The soldiers came from a variety of CMFs: engineering, field artillery (FA), signals, intelligence, adjutant general, medical, and quartermaster. Although the soldiers were assigned to different units, they were all stationed at the same base. Rather than using the ALRM as a framework from which to ask questions, we posed open-ended questions to the soldiers to solicit personal response rather than using the ALRM as a framework from which to ask questions. Appendix C details the interview protocol. Additionally, the interviews were conducted in person and were done one-on-one to limit the influence of responses from others.

Although the sample was very small, the responses consistently identified the same qualities associated with Army leadership. Three themes in particular were frequently mentioned: leaders who cared about their soldiers, leaders who effectively trained their

Table 4.1
Army Leadership According to Qualitative Interviews

	Caring	Educator	Knowledgeable
Fraction of respondents who mentioned theme	13 of 19	6 of 19	10 of 19
Example descriptions of effective leader	"Supportive and caring" "Worried about my welfare" "Took care of soldiers" "Spoke up for [respondent]" "Social support"	"Mentors soldiers" "Teaches across ranks and levels" "Passionate about training future leaders"	"Demonstrated and set the standard" "Knowledgeable and flexible"
Example descriptions of ineffective leader	"Mission first and doesn't care about the soldiers" "Professional disrespect"	"Has no desire to train or mentor"	"Very incompetent" "Doesn't lead by example"

NOTE: Qualitative interviews.

soldiers, and leaders who were knowledgeable. Table 4.1 provides example responses from the soldiers and how they align with the three themes. The table shows how those characteristics were ascribed to effective leaders or lacking in ineffective leaders.

The characteristics of effective leadership described by soldiers interviewed aligned well with Army doctrine. Returning to the ALRM attributes and competencies, the themes of caring, educating, and knowledge are also present. Table 4.2 shows the alignment of the ALRM with the themes from the qualitative interviews.

Table 4.2
Army Leadership Qualities from Qualitative Interviews Aligned to the Army Leadership Requirements Model

	Caring	Educator	Knowledgeable
ALRM attribute	Empathizes		Has expertise
ALRM competency	Builds trust Communicates Creates a positive environment Has interpersonal tact	Prepares self Develops others	Gets results Leads by example

NOTE: Qualitative interviews.

Given the consistency between Army doctrine and soldier assessments of effective leadership, we then set out to determine whether the Army promotes personnel based on those characteristics.

Army Doctrine Defines Promotion Requirements

AR 600-8-19 prescribes policies and procedures governing promotions and reductions of Army enlisted personnel (HQDA, 2017). Promotions to E-2, E-3, and E-4 are part of the decentralized promotion system and are governed primarily by eligibility criteria and TIS and TIG requirements. The E-5 and E-6 promotion system is considered semicentralized. For promotion to E-5, a soldier is required to have at least 18 months TIS and six months TIG. The semicentralized promotion system aims to fill authorized enlisted positions with the best-qualified soldiers that meet a minimum number of promotion points for their MOSs. Soldiers earn promotion points as a result of information contained in their personnel and training records. For example, points are allotted based on combat experience, performance on weapon qualification, and the Army physical fitness test (APFT). Additionally, points can be earned from awards and decorations and military or civilian education. For promotion to E-5, a maximum of 800 points are available. Figure 4.2 shows the point allocation across the different criteria.

Figure 4.3 illustrates the relative weighting of promotion points for E-5 and E-6 promotions.

Centralized promotions to E-7, E-8, and E-9 are based on demonstrated performance in present and lower ranks and *potential ability* at the higher rank (U.S. Army Human Resources Command, 2015b). Centralized boards convene to select soldiers for promotion to those ranks, and NCOERs are submitted to this board. The NCOER was recently revamped to reflect the current leadership doctrine (i.e., ADRP 6-22) (U.S. Army Human Resources Command, 2015a). As a result, the NCOER does a better job than the promotion point process does assessing the relevant attributes and competencies desired of Army leadership. Table 4.3 itemizes the Army values, attributes, skills, and actions evaluated in the NCOER.

The Early Promotion Process Does Not Reflect Leadership Requirements

Table 4.4 maps the ALRM attributes and competencies to the promotion point categories for E-5 and E-6. As the table illustrates, the promotion point process does little to capture many of the attributes and competencies required of an Army leader. At most, AR 600-8-19 states, only soldiers "who are competent in their current rank who show

Figure 4.2
Army Promotion Point Allocation to E-5 and E-6

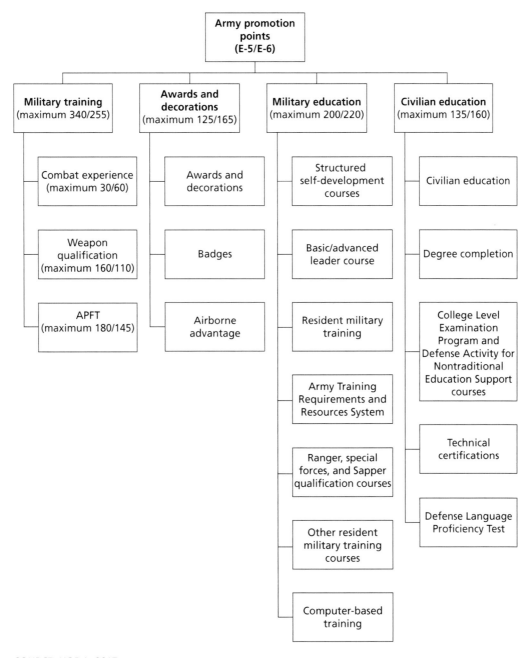

SOURCE: HQDA, 2017.
RAND *RR2211-4.2*

Figure 4.3
Relative Weighting for Promotion Points

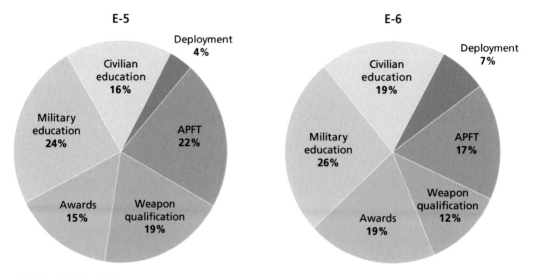

SOURCE: HQDA, 2017.

RAND RR2211-4.3

Table 4.3
Army Values, Attributes, Skills, and Actions Evaluated in the Noncommissioned Officer Education System

Value	Competence	Fitness	Leadership	Training	Responsibility
Loyalty	Duty proficiency	Mental and physical toughness	Mission first	Individual and team	Care and maintenance of equipment
Duty	Technical and tactical	Endurance	Genuine concern for soldiers	Mission focused	Soldier and equipment safety
Respect	Sound judgment	Looks like a soldier	Instill the spirit to achieve and win	Teaching soldiers	Conservation of supplies
Selfless service	Seeking self-improvement		Set the example	Sharing knowledge and experience	Encourage soldiers to learn and grow
Honor	Committed to excellence				Responsible for good, bad, right, and wrong
Integrity					
Personal courage					

SOURCE: HQDA, 2015c.

Table 4.4
Promotion Point Categories Mapping to the Army Leadership Requirements Model

ALRM Attribute	Promotion Point Category	ALRM Competency	Promotion Point Category
Army values		Leads others	Deployment experience
Empathy		Builds trust	
Warrior ethos		Extends influence	
Military bearing		Leads by example	
Fitness	APFT	Communicates	
Confidence		Creates positive environment	
Resilience		Prepares self	Military and civilian educations
Mental agility		Develops others	
Sound judgment		Stewardship	
Innovation		Gets results	Awards and decorations
Interpersonal tact			
Expertise	Weapon qualification Deployment experience		

potential to serve at positions of increased responsibility will be recommended for pro-motion to the next higher rank" (HQDA, 2017, p. 22).

The promotion point process captures largely the knowledge theme when referring to the leadership qualities identified in our interviews. Deployment experience, civilian education, awards, and weapon qualification might serve as proxies for effective leader-ship, but they are indirect. For example, in a longitudinal study of cadets, Atwater et al. (1999) found that actual physical fitness was one of only two variables that significantly predicted leadership emergence and leadership effectiveness. However, none of the fac-tors considered in promotion point process explicitly captures whether the NCO cares for his or her soldiers or is successful at mentoring and training them.[1]

Notably, a full 40 percent of promotion points to E-5 are associated with physi-cal fitness and weapons qualification. Certainly, standards for these outcomes should be met, but none of the soldiers we interviewed considered fitness or weapon expertise

---

[1] Since 2009, the Army has conducted an annual survey on Army leadership. Since the surveys began, soldiers have consistently reported that their immediate superior underperformed with respect to mentoring. In the 2013 survey, 20 percent of leaders reported that formal and informal performance counseling never or almost never occurs. Only about one-half agreed that performance counseling was useful for setting goals when it was done.

reflective of effective leadership skills.[2] Again, although weapon expertise may be a proxy for job knowledge, the relative allocation seems disproportionate to some of the other themes described in the interviews or attributes and competencies detailed in the ALRM.

It is not until a soldier is promoted to E-7 that the Army begins to consider whether the soldier has the desirable attributes and competencies of Army leadership. It is also the first instance in which the *potential* ability of the soldier is considered.

Recommendations for Improving the Promotion Process

Industrial and organizational psychology often separates job tasks into two categories—task performance and contextual activities (Borman and Motowidlo, 1997). Task performance can be defined as the effectiveness with which job incumbents perform activities that contribute to the organization's technical core either directly by implementing a part of its technological process or indirectly by providing it with needed materials or services. Contextual activities contribute to organizational effectiveness in ways that shape the organizational, social, and psychological context that serves as the catalyst for task activities and processes. Contextual performance can be further stratified into job dedication and interpersonal facilitation (Conway, 1999).

The qualities of effective leadership that the soldiers described included elements of both task performance and contextual activities. The knowledgeability theme aligns with task performance, whereas the caring theme aligns with contextual activities. The educator theme contains elements of both, as the interviewees described leaders not only training subordinates but also creating a learning environment to help them be successful.

The Army should consider how to capture such qualities as compassion and fostering a learning environment when promoting soldiers to E-5 and E-6. Borman and Motowidlo (1997, p. 107) stated that "when contextual performance dimensions are included as criteria, personality predictors are more likely to be successful correlates." The Army should not only be considering soldiers' historical demonstration of leadership in the promotion process but also be considering the *potential* for leadership, as it does for senior NCO positions. Measures of personality traits in the form of quantitative personality tests could be used to predict who is likely to be effective in terms of contextual performance, although this would involve additional research to determine the relationship between proposed measures and leadership potential/ effectiveness. The recommendation is compatible with other Army initiatives, such as the U.S. Army Human Dimension Concept (Department of the Army, 2014a). Addi-

---

[2]   Our interviews did not include infantrymen. Those soldiers may weigh physical fitness or weapon expertise higher than those at the MOS interviewed did. But even if they were to consider those qualities for expert leadership, infantrymen reflect only a minority of the Army as a whole despite being the largest MOS.

tionally, the Army could adopt a variant of the 360-degree feedback process that is popular in the private sector, in which subordinates, peers, and superiors are asked to rate the soldier. This could be especially helpful, as it is likely that only those who know the soldier would be able to assess that soldier's compassion. For example, commanders and peers can speak to a soldier's competence, military bearing, and responsibility, whereas a subordinate can speak to a soldier's compassion and leadership ability. These assessments could translate into additional points in the promotion process.

Additionally, given that senior leaders with experience—both in deployment and YOSs—have lower attrition rates of soldiers they command, it is notable that there is relatively little weighting in the promotion point process for that type of experience. For example, deployment experience maximally accounts for between 4 percent and 8 percent of the promotion points. The Army may want to consider capturing that leadership experience more completely in the promotion of junior enlisted personnel.

Concluding Observations on the Army Promotion Process

The data suggest that experience matters in senior leaders; however, the Army promotion process captures only a limited amount of that experience since it considers deployment experience solely when promoting to E-5 and E-6. Additionally, Army doctrine and interviews with junior enlisted personnel identify multiple competencies and attributes associated with effective leadership, none of which is explicitly captured in the promotion process until promotion to E-7. These observations suggest that the Army is not identifying soldiers with leadership potential early in their careers and fostering them accordingly. These soldiers may be identified as part of an informal process of mentoring in the NCO support channels, but, doctrinally, the Army's process is not oriented to identify those soldiers as a matter of course. As a result, the Army may be losing effective leaders early and limiting the pool of senior NCOs.

CHAPTER FIVE

Which Soldiers Does the Army Retain?

Since the draft was abolished and the All-Volunteer Force was established in 1973, policymakers and researchers have focused on recruiting and retaining a professional military force. The Army allocated more than $4 billion in FY 2015 for recruiting and training alone (Office of the Under Secretary of Defense [Comptroller]/Chief Financial Officer, 2015). Given the hefty costs associated with these activities, there is a substantial body of research focused on whether enlisted personnel complete the initial term of service.

Most relevant for this study is a series of reports that develop measures of performance based on education, test scores, and early-career promotion speed (Ward and Tan, 1985; Hosek and Mattock, 2003; Asch, Romley, and Totten, 2005). As a group, these reports argue persuasively that speed of promotion is a measure of performance and that this measure includes information not revealed by test scores or education credentials (possibly this information is related to effort or job match). These reports find that the personnel retained are fast promoters and thus are of higher quality than average. Essentially, this research indicates that the services' promotion processes are effective at rewarding and thus helping to retain the most-effective personnel. However, these analyses differ from what we present here in several fundamental ways: Two of the reports focus on the first term, and all of these reports analyze data from all four services, quantify fast promoters as all who promote faster than average, and include accessions in an earlier period (1979–1992). Finally, the methodology differs fundamentally from what we present here, and these reports do not adjust for measures of leadership. For these reasons, it is not exactly clear how to compare our results; any of the above factors could cause differences, although the differing methodologies seem a particularly likely factor.

Our results suggest that several characteristics of senior leaders are associated with junior performance within the first 36 months. In particular, junior attrition is lower in units in which the senior leaders have more experience (up to a limit); attrition in units of senior leaders who promoted more quickly than most to E-6 is higher than in other similar units. In this chapter, we examine longer-term measures of retention across an Army career to determine the overall continuation rates of personnel who stay beyond the first reenlistment and to determine which leaders the Army retains.

Speed of Promotion over Time

The results outlined in Chapter Three suggest that the fastest promoters are not always the best leaders. However, evidence suggests that fast promoters are high-performing soldiers during the early portions of their careers. Also, by the time we observe promotion of soldiers to E-6, E-7, and beyond, many soldiers of their original cohorts have completed their initial terms and have left the Army. For these reasons, we maintain an interest in determining whether fast-promoting soldiers are more or less likely than other soldiers to be retained.[1] We explore this question in more detail here.

Soldiers can be divided into three promotion groups when using TIS as our metric: those who promote faster than most of their peers, those who promote slower than most of their peers, and those who promote at roughly the average speed. After careful consideration, a 15–70–15-percent split was chosen because it provided strong levels of discrimination between groups while also providing sufficiently large samples. Thus, going forward, the performance categories reflect the fastest 15 percent, the middle 70 percent, and the slowest 15 percent in terms of TIS to their promotion to the rank of E-5 and E-6. Promotion speed is calculated from the point of the prior promotion; thus, promotion speed to E-7 is calculated from the time the soldier was promoted to E-6.

We find that the median promotion time to E-5 decreased over the time period included in our sample. However, we find that, across the sample, initial fast promotion predicts later fast promotion; those who are promoted quickly to E-5 also tend to be promoted quickly to E-6 and E-7. Figure 5.1 shows this for infantry personnel; the trend holds across other CMFs as well.

Figure 5.1 should be read from left to right: The first set of columns demonstrates that those who are promoted fastest to E-6 were often promoted fast to E-5 (about 45 percent of the fast promoters to E-6 were promoted fast to E-5). Slow promoters to E-6 were most often—nearly 70 percent of the time—slow promoters to E-5 as well (third set of columns). Those who promoted around the median speed to E-5 often promoted around the median speed to E-6 (the second set of columns indicates that more than 80 percent of median promoters to E-6 were also median promoters to E-5).[2]

This figure shows two trends: First, E-5 promotion speed is highly correlated with later promotion speed, and this is especially true with median and slow promoters.

---

[1]   As noted in the beginning of this chapter, Asch, Romley, and Totten (2005) examined a similar question—but they did so using a different methodology (a quality index), and they examine cross-service data from cohorts who entered in FYs 1978–1991. Asch, Romley, and Totten found that higher-quality personnel are more likely to be retained and promoted, *but* they noted that many of their results hold only for the earlier cohorts (see, for example, Table S.1 in Asch, Romley, and Totten, 2005.

[2]   We also tested the correlations between the indicators of fast and slow promotion. As we might expect, fast promotions to E-6, E-7, and E-8 are highly correlated; promotions to adjacent ranks are more highly correlated than those that are separated by a rank. Slow promotion times are less highly correlated, and, in some cases, these correlations are not statistically significant, perhaps reflecting the tendency for slow promoters to leave the Army.

Figure 5.1
Promotion Speed, by Performance Group (Infantry)

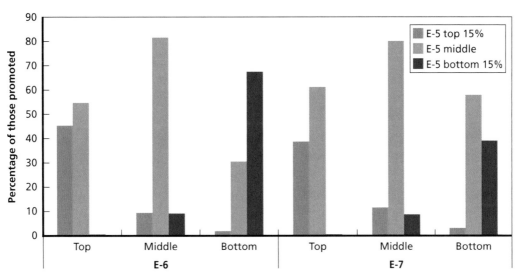

SOURCE: RAND Arroyo Center Analysis of TAPDB and DMDC data.
RAND RR2211-5.1

However, many who were promoted fastest to E-6 and E-7 were not among the fastest promoters to E-5; this is because a substantial number of those who promoted quickly to E-5 left the Army prior to reaching later milestones. We note that TIS requirements could explain part of this result. Next, we explore this trend in more detail.

Many factors are likely to influence promotion and promotion speed. For example, the Army's needs, which varied markedly over the time period, are an important factor in promotion speed. Therefore, we ran a series of regression models that examined the probabilities of being promoted quickly (compared with peers) and of being promoted at all. Consistently, being promoted quickly to E-5 is a strong predictor of subsequent promotions and of subsequent promotion speed; those who were promoted quickly to E-5 are more likely to be promoted (and to be promoted quickly) to E-6, E-7, and E-8. This is true when holding constant personal characteristics (gender, ethnicity, education level, AFQT score, age at entry), as well as FY and quarter of entry. Likewise, fast promotion to E-6 (calculated from the point at which the soldier became an E-5) predicts future promotion and promotion speed. Fast promotion to E-7 also predicts subsequent promotions. In summary, the promotion process is very consistent; those who are promoted quickly through earlier ranks are likely to be promoted into the senior ranks and are likely to arrive there ahead of their peers. However, being promoted requires remaining in the Army. These findings are consistent with those found in the series of reports that developed quality measures of performance based on education, test scores, and early-career promotion speed (Ward and Tan, 1985; Hosek and Mattock, 2003; Asch, Romley, and Totten, 2005). All of these sources include some evidence of a person-specific component that persists through time and represents the capacity to be promoted more quickly than one's peers. The authors of these papers generally found that this component is related to the capacity to be an effective service member, but none of these reports examines the influence of leaders on followers. Here, we found that the fastest-promoted leaders are not always the most effective, although it is quite possible that fast promoters grow into effective leaders (and perhaps even do so at the same rate as other leaders).

The Army Does Not Retain All Fast Promoters

Figure 5.2 presents continuation rates of soldiers who completed at least 36 months of service, divided by speed of E-5 promotion. In Figure 5.2, *fast promotion* is defined as being among the top 15 percent of those promoted, by FY of enlistment; *slow promotion* is defined as being among the 15 percent who were promoted most slowly by FY of enlistment. *Medium* includes the 70 percent who fall in neither the fast nor the slow category. Figure 5.2 indicates that continuation is higher among those promoted more slowly to E-5, but it also indicates that the differences emerge between 48 and 60 months and remain mostly stable over most of the following years. In other words, soldiers who promote quickly to E-5 are more likely than others to leave at the first

Figure 5.2
Continuation Rates, by E-5 Promotion Speed

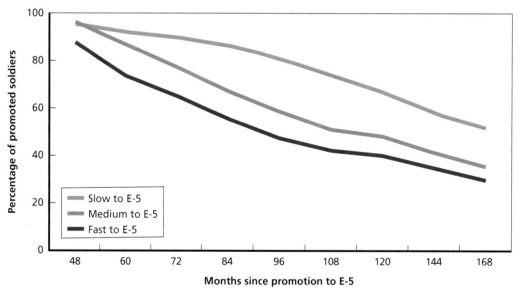

SOURCE: RAND Arroyo Center Analysis of TAPDB and DMDC data.

reenlistment point.[3] The continuation rate of those who are promoted more slowly to E-5 is higher than that of the others, especially over the second term.

The pattern differs somewhat at the E-6 promotion point (not shown). This is because the variation in time to E-6 is substantial; soldiers who promote relatively slowly to E-6 often spend at least five years as E-5s. Thus, achieving this promotion requires high levels of continuation; soldiers who would have promoted relatively slowly to E-6 could leave the Army after eight more YOSs without achieving the E-6 promotion. However, conditionally on remaining in the Army for at least 36 or 48 months, those who promote quickly to E-6 have a high likelihood of future retention.

Next, to ensure that these results are not driven by changes in Army policy over time or by changes in the characteristics of soldiers over time, we modeled continuation much as we did in the previous chapter. Here, we again limited our sample to those who complete at least 36 months. Because of the longer and more complicated nature of NCO careers, we do not match soldiers with leaders throughout their careers (as discussed earlier, other evidence suggests that leadership may be especially important in the early phases of a career). However, we do include personal characteristics, as well as indicators of the FY of accession, time deployed in the first term, and an indicator for fast promotion (to E-5 or E-6). We estimated a series of models examining the probability of continuation from 60 to 120 months.

Consistent with our earlier results, our regression results indicate that personal characteristics are associated with continuation; for example, women have lower continuation rates than men (although the differences are smaller than during the first term). Continuation rates vary with FY of entry. Deployment experience in the first 48 months generally has a very small and insignificant relationship with continuation. Soldiers who lack traditional high school diplomas, as well as those who scored below 92 on the AFQT, have *higher* rates of continuation than other soldiers.

When we examine continuation as a function of promotion speed to E-5, we find that fast promotion to E-5 is associated with somewhat lower continuation rates throughout the second term (this is consistent with the data in Figure 5.2). Finally, faster promotion to E-6 is associated with substantially higher continuation.

In summary, continuation rates differ somewhat by promotion speed. Those who promote quickly to E-5 have somewhat lower continuation rates than other soldiers, but some of this difference also occurs at the end of the first term. In contrast, those who promote quickly to E-6 have higher continuation rates than other similar soldiers; E-6 promotion appears to be a signal of both the Army's commitment to the soldier and the soldier's commitment to the Army. Our results suggest that the Army does not retain many who promote quickly during the first term but is more successful in retaining the soldiers who promote quickly to E-6. Despite the fact that many of those

---

[3] While this appears to run contrary to the findings of Hosek and Mattock (2003), recall that these authors emphasized performance only within the first 48 months.

who promote quickly to E-5 leave the Army, it is also worth noting that speed of promotion is highly correlated throughout the career for those who remain in the Army; the soldiers who promote quickly to E-6 or E-7 were, in many cases, among those who promoted quickly to E-5.

Concluding Observations on Retaining Fast Promoters

The data indicate that there are some leadership attributes that encourage retention of soldiers, based on the results in Chapter Three. In particular, attrition is higher in units with leaders who were fast promoters and thus have less experience. We demonstrate that soldiers who are promoted quickly in the early parts of their careers tend to be among those promoted quickly to higher pay grades. Our results also indicate that many of these fastest promoters leave the Army. Do note that our model focuses on *only* promotion time; as discussed, the quality index models differ from the straightforward models we run here, and the results from such models suggest that the services effectively retain many of those who promote quickly during the early years of their careers. Comparing results across these models would provide additional insights into the workings of the Army's promotion and retention systems.

Retaining fast promoters may be a worthy goal; they are likely to perform strongly on many measures. However, from the perspective of managing unit attrition, it is not clear that the fastest promoters make the most-effective unit leaders, or perhaps these fast promoters require more time to become effective unit leaders. Indeed, experience obtained by those who promote more slowly seems to have a positive effect on junior soldier performance. Thus, from the perspective of managing attrition, retaining soldiers who promote in the median range makes the most sense. Of course, it may be possible to provide additional training or experience to the fastest-promoting soldiers prior to putting them in charge of units. Finally, it seems likely that considering the potential for leadership earlier in the promotion process (e.g., at the E-5 or E-6 promotions, as discussed in Chapter Four) could result in more-effective leadership, regardless of how quickly the leader was promoted.

CHAPTER SIX

Conclusions and Implications

Experienced Leadership Is Valuable

Using the results of our data analysis, we can begin to quantify the value of senior leader experience. In particular, for a given soldier with baseline individual and institutional characteristics, we can examine how different leadership characteristics might affect that soldier's likelihood of attrition.

Many of our measures of senior leader experience covary with one another. For example, leaders who promoted quickly to E-6 will have fewer years in service on average than leaders who promoted more slowly. While regression analysis is a powerful tool for isolating the relationships of multiple variables, interpreting the overall value of experience requires considering the total effect of the factors that are likely to covary. To do this, we use our data to determine the extent to which our primary measures of experience covary among senior enlisted personnel. We considered the overall effects of three representative leaders on the likelihood of attrition of a soldier with the same individual and institutional characteristics. Each leader's other characteristics (such as AFQT score) match those of the median or typical leader. We use our regression results to calculate the probability of 36-month failure-to-adapt attrition for a typical soldier, allowing only leader characteristics to vary. We assigned our typical soldier the median characteristics of a junior soldier in our sample—white male with an AFQT score of 56, high school diploma, and age 18–19 at enlistment.

Table 6.1 details those characteristics and the resulting likelihood that the soldier will leave the Army before 36 months. The predicted likelihood of attrition varies; our results indicate that attrition is expected to be more than 2 percentage points *higher* in the unit with the less experienced leader. It is the combination of speedy promotion to E-6 and overall low level of TIS that creates this sizable effect; when we vary other characteristics, such as leader time deployed, we find very small predicted differences in attrition. Having a leader who is new to the unit is also associated with a higher attrition rate; the difference is a bit more than 1 percentage point between units with new leaders and similar units with leaders who have been in the units for at least 15 months.

Table 6.1
Attrition Rates of Soldiers with Varying Leadership Experience

Senior Leader Characteristic	Junior Soldier Characteristic	Likelihood That a Soldier Will Leave the Army Before 36 Months
Fast to promote to E-6	White male	14.4 percent (high attrition)
Less than 22 years in the Army	High school graduate	
Total deployment experience of 20–40 months	Enlisted at age 18–19	
	AFQT cat IIIB	
Least experienced	Combat arms CMF	
	Not yet deployed	
Average time to E-6	White male	12.4 percent (low attrition)
22–25 years in the Army	High school graduate	
Total deployment experience of 20–40 months	Enlisted at age 18–19	
	AFQT cat IIIB	
	Combat arms CMF	
	Not yet deployed	
Slow to promote to E-6	White male	13.4 percent (medium attrition)
More than 25 years in the Army	High school graduate	
Total deployment experience of 20–40 months	Enlisted at age 18–19	
	AFQT cat IIIB	
Most experienced	Combat arms CMF	
	Not yet deployed	

Leadership experience affects both the promotion and retention rates of subordinates. Having a leader with the right mix of experience can potentially save the Army a substantial sum on an annual basis. We compared the predicted attrition rates in two similar units that differ only in terms of senior experience to roughly estimate the potential savings. We considered a relatively small unit with 100 junior soldiers. Our regression results indicate that such a unit would be expected to have an attrition rate between 12.4 percent and 14.4 percent, depending on the leadership characteristics. Attrition would be expected to differ by one to two soldiers (1–2 percent) based on experience; we would expect attrition to be 2 percent higher in a unit with a less experienced leader than in a unit with a leader of more typical experience.

The attrition of our focus—36-month failure-to-adapt attrition—typically occurs between 18 and 24 months of service. Thus, lowering attrition by 1–2 percentage points would mean that one to two additional soldiers would complete initial terms, rather than leaving approximately two years prior to completing the term. Thus, senior experience could be expected to translate into two to four additional YOSs. This suggests that the Army would need to recruit between one-half and one fewer soldiers for each unit with a leader of typical experience than with a less experienced leader.

Recruiting and training are expensive; recent estimates suggest that recruiting and training one soldier costs roughly $60,000 to $70,000 (Office of the Deputy Assistant Secretary of the Army for Cost and Economics, 2015). This suggests that having a more experienced leader could translate into cost savings of $30,000 to $60,000. Of course, more-experienced leaders also require higher pay. While there are many ways to calculate the cost of a soldier, pay differences at the more experienced end of the enlisted career are relatively modest. For example, an E-9 with 22 YOSs costs the Army approximately $100,000 per year, while an E-9 with 24 YOSs costs the Army roughly $102,000 per year.[1] Pay grade differences are larger than those calculated solely on YOSs; an E-9 costs roughly $15,000 more than an E-8. These rough calculations suggest that the difference in cost between the least experienced leaders and leaders with more typical levels of experience is more than offset by the savings associated with lower levels of attrition in the unit with a leader with a typical level of experience. In contrast, the most experienced leaders are more costly than leaders with more typical levels of experience, and their units are expected to have slightly higher attrition.

Another noteworthy finding is that attrition is higher at times when the leader is new to the unit, regardless of the leader's experience level. In our data, about one-third of leaders have fewer than 15 months of experience in their current units. This suggests that a leader's start-up period is expensive to the Army. There may be ways to maintain continuity—perhaps by designing a substantial overlap between leaders at times of transition, perhaps by increasing the length of time a soldier spends in a leadership position in a specific unit, or perhaps through other mechanisms. Our results suggest that focusing on this issue also has the potential for cost savings.

These calculations must be caveated in a couple of ways: They are conservative in that they are for a unit with a relatively small number of junior personnel, and we assumed no additional service beyond the first term. However, we note that the calculations assigned all of the difference in attrition to the leader of the unit, which is likely to be inaccurate. Our estimates based on identifying leaders in various ways (i.e., by four-, five-, or six-digit UIC) indicate that leaders at various levels can and do influence attrition. Therefore, the observed attrition differences may be thought of as partly due to the experience of those below the senior leader level. Finally, above and beyond differences in attrition, leadership is likely to have other impacts on how a unit functions (this was suggested by our qualitative work); in this case, our attrition differences likely

---

[1] Costs were calculated using Regular Military Compensation, which includes basic pay, housing allowance, tax advantage, and basic allowance for subsistence. Our compensation estimates are for married personnel who live in the Fort Hood area; estimates are from the Regular Military Compensation calculator (U.S. Department of Defense, undated).

understate the true value of experience. Finally, our analyses assumed that leaders are assigned to units randomly. If, in fact, the most-effective leaders are assigned to the most difficult units (where *difficult* is related to low retention), our results could understate the true value of experience for this reason. Regardless, our estimates suggest that leadership does have value, that attrition is higher in units with less experienced leaders, and that the difference in attrition rates is likely to outweigh the additional cost associated with having a more experienced senior leader and is likely to counteract at least some of the cost of having a more experienced leadership team throughout the unit.

The Army Can Control for Quality of Leadership Throughout a Career

Unlike individual or institutional characteristics, which the Army can only control for once at the start of an enlisted career, promoting soldiers with the right leadership skills is a continual process over which the Army has control as part of its regulations and processes.

Early-term promotions are generally automatic and occur on a highly predictable timetable. When promoting a soldier to E-5 or E-6, many factors are considered, including military training, military education, civilian education, awards, decorations, and achievements. Although unit commanders implicitly capture leadership *potential* when recommending junior soldiers for promotion, it is not until promotion to E-7 and higher that the Army begins to explicitly consider a soldier's demonstrated leadership as part of the promotion process.

The Army promotion process is not actively identifying effective leaders, and the promotion point process is largely not consistent with identifying soldiers with the Army-defined characteristics of effective leaders. As a result, although "fast promoters" may be excellent soldiers, fast promotion does not imply that they are also excellent leaders. Given this, despite the Army's low retention of fast promoters, improving retention may not actually improve outcomes among junior enlisted personnel. Instead, the Army should consider altering the point allocation in the promotion process to capture the desired leadership qualities.

Examining other samples or other aspects of leadership could yield additional insights. For example, our decision to focus on MTOE units meant that women are underrepresented in our sample. But especially as women move in to more leadership positions in the combat arms–like occupations, exploring the extent to which gender influences aspects of leadership could yield helpful implications. And there are many more areas of potentially fruitful research surrounding leadership—for example, leadership styles may explain retention of junior personnel.

The Army Should Consider Ways to Identify and Promote Effective Leaders

As previously described, there is value to experienced leadership. The Army should consider ways to account for TIS or TIG in promotions so as to capture those benefits. The minimum and maximum service requirements appear to be insufficiently capturing this, as there is no correlation of fast promoters in senior leadership with fast promotion among subordinates and small correlation with reducing attrition. We note that it is not clear *why* fast-promoting senior leaders manage units with higher attrition. Given the variation in our data, there is no reason to think that fast-promoting leaders are necessarily poor leaders; rather, our results more likely suggest that the fastest-promoting leaders have not yet become strong leaders. It is also possible that fast-promoting leaders are, in some fundamental manner, more demanding as leaders; however, in this case, we might expect that soldiers serving under these leaders were themselves more likely to be promoted quickly. But this is not the case, as is shown in Figure 3.5 in Chapter Three.

In contrast, units with leaders who have unusually low or unusually high number of YOSs have both higher levels of attrition *and* higher levels of promotion. While this could be a simple relationship in which the probability of promotion is driven by the smaller number competing (a side effect of the higher attrition rate), we suspect that this is not the case, as personnel frequently switch locations prior to promotion and the effect sizes do not appear large enough to dramatically change the probability of promotion. Another interpretation is that unit leaders with unusually high or low numbers of YOSs are more-demanding leaders, resulting in higher attrition *and* higher promotion rates. It is not clear whether this is optimal from the Army's perspective.

Since the NCOER is derived from Army doctrine, it likely assesses leadership better than the promotion point process does. The Army may want to consider some elements of the NCOER earlier in the promotion pipeline to identify and encourage soldiers who demonstrate leadership potential. One approach would be to consider promotion exams to identify knowledgeable soldiers and those proficient in their MOS. Additionally, there may be value in considering additional personality traits.

Of course, making changes to the promotion process to, for example, require more experience prior to taking a unit leadership role could have implications both for the Army and for individual soldiers. For example, requiring additional experience could discourage the fastest-promoting soldiers, as well as change the promotion paths of those who go on to the most-senior positions. In short, such changes should be made only after obtaining a more complete understanding of all of the trade-offs involved. In particular, although our analyses and the costs of recruiting and training soldiers suggest that attrition has costs and that experience has monetary value for the Army, this research does *not* determine the optimal level of attrition. Determining the optimal level of attrition to maximize the Army's performance would provide valuable information to determine the preferred levels of experience and promotion processes.

Potential Extensions to These Analyses

When modeling leader experience, we focused on only the most senior enlisted soldier in each unit. We did not explicitly model pathways through which leader experience influences junior soldiers. One potential pathway involves the midgrade NCOs in the unit; it is possible that a leader with an optimal level of experience is better able to develop the leadership skills in midgrade NCOs. If this is the case, the experience and characteristics of the midgrade NCOs may also be predictive of junior soldier attrition. Identifying the relationship between junior soldiers, midgrade NCOs, and senior enlisted leaders presents an additional empirical challenge; in some cases, information provided on NCOERs could assist in determining the reporting structures within units. Such information is currently unavailable to researchers.

Additionally, the match between leaders and followers on key characteristics may matter—for example, leaders who are of the same gender or who work in the same CMF may have more influence on the junior soldiers they lead. Our current data set had too few female leaders to test this hypothesis, but exploring these relationships could be a fruitful area for future research. Our results also indicate that attrition rates vary by base, even controlling for soldier and leader characteristics. This could indicate that base-level command climate is a key factor in explaining outcomes or that characteristics of the area around the base matter. Future research could explore these differences as well. Finally, while we controlled for the time that the senior leader spent in the unit, we lack a direct measure of the amount of time that each junior soldier was exposed to each senior leader.

Our model is straightforward in the sense that we focused on the individual soldier and control for base- and leader-specific attributes. In doing so, we made several inherent assumptions. In particular, this model assumed that leader characteristics do not influence soldier characteristics (this is most likely valid, as most of the soldier characteristics we included were measured at enlistment). However, our model also assumed that base characteristics do not influence leader characteristics. This assumption could be invalid if, for example, leaders with certain levels of experience are more likely to be assigned to certain bases (perhaps because of their CMFs). One way to deal with this issue is to use a hierarchical model; the value-added models commonly used to estimate the effects of school and teacher characteristics on student outcomes, provide some guidance (for a review of these models, see Koedel, Mihaly, and Rockoff, 2015). Future work could explore the application of such models to Army data; these models could provide additional insights.

In summary, our results indicate that specific leader traits are correlated with first-term performance of junior enlisted soldiers. Consistent with prior research is that the traits of the soldiers themselves (education, age at enlistment, AFQT score) are strongly related to attrition; however, even when we hold these factors constant, senior enlisted experience appears to matter in a fashion that suggests that experience can be quite valuable.

The Empirical Model and Regression Results

The Empirical Model

We posited that there are multiple factors that influence soldier attrition, continuation, promotion, and demotion; consequently, we modeled each outcome as a function of individual, institutional, and leadership factors. We defined our empirical model as follows:

$$Y_i = \alpha + \beta X_i + \gamma I_j + \delta L_k + \varepsilon_{ijk} \quad ,$$

where
- Y_i = the outcome of interest for an enlisted soldier (depending on the model, the outcome is attrition or continuation at 36 and 48 months, fast promotion to E-5, or demotion within 24 months of E-5 promotion)
- X_i = the vector of soldier individual characteristics, including gender, race, education, AFQT score, age at enlistment, deployment experience, and year and quarter of enlistment
- I_j = a set of institutional-level characteristics, such as the location
- L_k = a set of senior leader characteristics, which includes various measures of senior leader experience (deployment experience, TIS, time in unit, speed of promotion)
- ε_{ijk} = the error term.

To estimate this model, we applied logistic regression techniques to account for the dichotomous nature of our outcome variables. The regression coefficients are non-linear; for this reason, we present marginal effects of each variable in the text. As part of our empirical strategy, we developed and tested different specifications of the model; in particular, we defined some of our variables as categories as well as in continuous terms and included square terms and interactions to test the stability of the coefficient estimates.[1] We also developed several alternative methods of identifying the leader in each unit. While our primary methodology identifies the senior leader in the unit through company assignment and job titles, we also developed and tested several more-straightforward ways of identifying the leader in each unit. Specifically, we used only the (four-, five- or six-digit) UIC to identify the most senior person in each unit and assumed that person was the leader. In the final subsection of this appendix, we present some of the results produced by this alternative methodology; they are broadly similar to the results produced by our primary methodology. Next, we describe our sample in more detail.

Data Set

To form our data set, we began by selecting enlisted personnel who entered the Regular Army in the years 2002–2014 (FYs 2002–2014, inclusive). We next selected personnel who successfully completed their initial training and were assigned to MTOE battalion-level units within 15 months of entering the Army. We used these criteria to create a roughly comparable sample of young soldiers at their first duty stations. By using these criteria, we excluded those who failed to complete their initial training (and thus, our attrition rates are lower than rates that include the entire early career). We are also excluding those who entered MOSs with excessively long training pipelines, as well as those who were not initially assigned to MTOE units. These exclusions cut out a substantial portion of young soldiers, but we did retain more than one-half of all young soldiers and a higher proportion of those in the combat arms professions (who are quite likely to be assigned to MTOE units).

Selecting on MTOE battalion-level units means that the units in our sample follow a traditional unit hierarchy; we used this hierarchy when developing our primary methodology for identifying leaders. Specifically, we identified the leader in each unit via duty titles (two members of the study team independently examined the duty titles; while there is some variation across duty titles, the team members were able to consistently identify the same leaders). In some units, duty titles were missing or unclear; in these cases, we identified the leader as the E-9 who had been in the unit longest and, in cases with no E-9 in the unit, we identified the E-8 who had been in the unit longest as the leader. Our results were consistent even when we excluded these "imputed" leaders. In some cases, there were multiple E-9s with the same duty title in a unit during the same month. In these cases, we used average values for the leadership measures.

---

[1]   Throughout these specifications, the parameter coefficients remain largely stable.

Descriptive Statistics

Our sample includes more than 200,000 soldiers who enlisted in FY 2002 or later and were assigned to MTOE units within the first 15 months after entering the Army. Our data also include information on the senior enlisted soldier at each unit (the unit leader). Table A.1 provides descriptive statistics on the sample, and Table A.2 shows the correlation of key leader characteristics.

Note that, when we examined 36-month attrition and continuation outcomes, we included only those soldiers who entered the Army early enough for us to observe their outcome over 36 months; when we examined 48-month attrition and continua-

Table A.1
Descriptive Statistics, Sample of Junior Personnel and Their Leaders

Variable	Mean	Minimum, Maximum	Standard Deviation
36-month failure-to-adapt attrition	0.133	0, 1	0.340
Fast promotion to E-5	0.318	0, 1	0.466
Demotion from E-5 (among E-5s)	0.061	0, 1	0.0239
48-month attrition	0.173	0, 1	0.378
36-month continuation	0.772	0, 1	0.420
48-month continuation	0.541	0, 1	0.498
Soldier characteristics			
Female	0.0553	0, 1	0.229
Non-Hispanic white	0.689	0, 1	0.463
African American	0.132	0, 1	0.339
Hispanic	0.125	0, 1	0.331
Other ethnicity	0.053	0, 1	0.224
Younger than 18 years of age at enlistment	0.043	0, 1	0.204
18–19 at enlistment	0.442	0, 1	0.497
20–22 at enlistment	0.308	0, 1	0.462
23 years old and older at enlistment	0.207	0, 1	0.405
High school graduate	0.759	0, 1	0.428
College	0.102	0, 1	0.302
General Educational Development (GED)	0.135	0, 1	0.342
No credential ("dropout")	0.0043	0, 1	0.065

Table A.1—Continued

Variable	Mean	Minimum, Maximum	Standard Deviation
AFQT cat I: 93–100	0.0508	0, 1	0.22
AFQT cat II: 65–92	0.336	0, 1	0.473
AFQT cat IIIA: 50–64	0.263	0, 1	0.44
AFQT cat IIIB: 31–49	0.333	0, 1	0.471
AFQT cat IV: Less than 30	0.0167	0, 1	0.128
Months deployed	11.0	0, 69	11.17
Leader characteristics			
E-8	0.2822	0,1	0.4502
E-9	0.7178	0,1	0.4502
Months deployed	23.2	0, 69	13.73
Less than 22 YOSs	0.168	0, 1	0.373
23–24 YOSs	0.450	0, 1	0.496
More than 25 YOSs	0.390	0 ,1	0.488
New to unit (less than 15 months)	0.342	0, 1	0.474
Fastest promotion to E-6	0.161	0, 1	0.367
AFQT cat I	0.0152	0, 1	0.222
AFQT cat II	0.287	0, 1	0.4523
AFQT cat IIIA	0.299	0, 1	0.4593
AFQT cat IIIB	0.633	0, 1	0.4819
AFQT cat IV	0.0676	0, 1	0.2511

Table A.2
Correlations of Key Senior Leader Characteristics

Characteristic	AFQT Score	Months Deployed	Months to E-6	Months in Army
AFQT score	–	–	–	–
Months deployed	0.1323***	–	–	–
Months to E-6	–0.0563***	0.0528***	–	–
Months in Army	–0.0850***	0.0967***	0.2888***	–
Months in MTOE unit	0.0376*	0.1086***	–0.0043	0.0267

NOTE: Pairwise correlations use the final observation on each senior enlisted leader. Stars indicate level of statistical significance: * 10 percent; ** 5 percent; *** 1 percent.

Table A.3
Regression Results: Attrition, Fast Promotion, and Demotion

Variable	36-Month Failure-to-Adapt Attrition	Promotion to E-5 Within 36 months	Demotion from E-5 Within 24 Months of Promotion
Soldier characteristics			
Women	0.633***	0.00345	−0.4410153***
	[0.570, 0.696]	[−0.0965, 0.103]	[−0.719, −0.163]
African American	0.240***	−0.179***	0.3987311***
	[0.192, 0.289]	[−0.242, −0.115]	[0.268, 0.529]
Hispanic	−0.289***	0.0107	0.070785
	[−0.342, −0.236]	[−0.0448, 0.0662]	[−0.059, 0.201]
Other	−0.226***	−0.0823*	0.082925
	[−0.305, −0.147]	[−0.162, −0.00215]	[−0.108, 0.274]
Age at enlistment			
Younger than 18	0.227***	−0.253***	0.1971592***
	[0.162, 0.291]	[−0.350, −0.157]	[0.0236, 0.370]
20–22	−0.191***	0.249***	−0.0947931*
	[−0.228, −0.153]	[0.206, 0.292]	[−0.196, 0.0068]
23 and older	−0.440***	0.534***	−0.3216428***
	[−0.487, −0.392]	[0.485, 0.582]	[−0.449, −0.194]
Education			
Dropout	0.633***	−0.716***	0.0672744
	[0.451, 0.815]	[−1.052, −0.381]	[−0.754, 0.888]
GED	0.594***	−0.175***	0.5038691***
	[0.553, 0.634]	[−0.231, −0.118]	[0.396, 0.611]
College or some college	−0.143***	0.600***	−0.0805751
	[−0.210, −0.0772]	[0.545, 0.654]	[−0.248, 0.087]
AFQT score			
AFQT cat I	−0.601***	0.495***	−0.589647***
	[−0.696, −0.506]	[0.419, 0.571]	[−0.827, −0.352]

Table A.3—Continued

Variable	36-Month Failure-to-Adapt Attrition	Promotion to E-5 Within 36 months	Demotion from E-5 Within 24 Months of Promotion
AFQT cat II	−0.269***	0.271***	−0.3270695***
	[−0.310, −0.229]	[0.224, 0.318]	[−0.438, −0.216]
AFQT cat IIIa	−0.0688***	0.127***	−0.1618046***
	[−0.109, −0.0288]	[0.0764, 0.178]	[−0.272, −0.0516]
AFQT cat IV	−0.046	−0.254***	−0.2076383
	[−0.161, 0.0690]	[−0.399, −0.109]	[−0.507, 0.0918]
Non−combat arms	−0.297***	−0.406***	0.0219102
	[−0.334, −0.260]	[−0.447, −0.366]	[−0.073, 0.117]
Deployment experience			
Deployed	−2.520***	−0.370***	
	[−2.571, −2.468]	[−0.409, −0.331]	
Deployed by E-5	–	–	0.0083655**
	–	–	[0.0022, 0.0145]
Leader characteristics			
Time in service or unit			
Less than 22 years	0.281***	0.0610*	−0.0011696
	[0.238, 0.323]	[0.0107, 0.111]	[−0.127, 0.124]
25 or more years	0.0905***	0.0775***	0.0784689
	[0.0512, 0.130]	[0.0343, 0.121]	[−0.026, 0.183]
Time in unit is less than 15 months	0.378***	0.0196	−0.0380204
	[0.344, 0.413]	[−0.0230, 0.0622]	[−0.142, 0.0656]
Promotion speed to E-6			
Fastest to E-6	0.0122	0.0000337	−0.0350685
	[−0.0434, 0.0678]	[−0.0636, 0.0636]	[−0.191, 0.121]
Second quartile to E-6	−0.253***	−0.0193	−0.0010774
	[−0.308, −0.198]	[−0.0807, 0.0421]	[−0.150, 0.148]
Third quartile to E-6	−0.199***	−0.00782	0.0303985
	[−0.275, −0.123]	[−0.0894, 0.0738]	[−0.166, 0.227]
Fourth quartile to E-6	−0.0478	−0.127***	0.0107188

Table A.3—Continued

Variable	36-Month Failure-to-Adapt Attrition	Promotion to E-5 Within 36 months	Demotion from E-5 Within 24 Months of Promotion
	[−0.110, 0.0146]	[−0.200, −0.0536]	[−0.159, 0.177]
AFQT score			
AFQT cat I	0.174*		−
	[0.0409, 0.307]	[−0.157, 0.230]	−
AFQT cat II	0.00189	−0.0324	−0.1540837***
	[−0.0389, 0.0427]	[−0.0787, 0.0139]	[−0.268, −0.0405]
AFQT cat IIIA	−0.175***	−0.0960***	−0.0781571
	[−0.216, −0.134]	[−0.140, −0.0515]	[−0.184, 0.0268]
AFQT cat IV	0.292***	0.0579	−0.1589583**
	[0.231, 0.353]	[−0.0165, 0.132]	[−0.326, 0.00793]
Senior deployment experience			
Not yet deployed	1.209***	0.193***	−0.1431871
	[1.124, 1.294]	[0.0888, 0.298]	[−0.347, 0.0609]
1–19 months	0.377***	0.103***	0.1243709***
	[0.334, 0.419]	[0.0537, 0.153]	[0.00556, 0.243]
More than 40 months	0.148***	−0.159***	0.0144434
	[0.0742, 0.222]	[−0.244, −0.0737]	[−0.237, 0.266]
Constant	−2.276***	−1.128***	−3.349852***
	[−2.390, −2.162]	[−1.261, −0.995]	[−3.676, −3.024]
Pseudo R-squared	0.174	0.059	0.0206

NOTE: Modeling promotion required a slightly different specification because the sample size was smaller. Stars indicate level of statistical significance: * 10 percent; ** 5 percent; *** 1 percent.

tion outcomes, we included only those soldiers who entered the Army early enough for us to observe their outcomes over 48 months.

Regression Results

Table A.3 shows our primary regression results. (These results are presented in Figures 3.4–3.12 in Chapter Three.) Table A.3 includes the estimated coefficients, as

Figure A.1
Probability of 36-Month Attrition as a Function of Soldier Traits

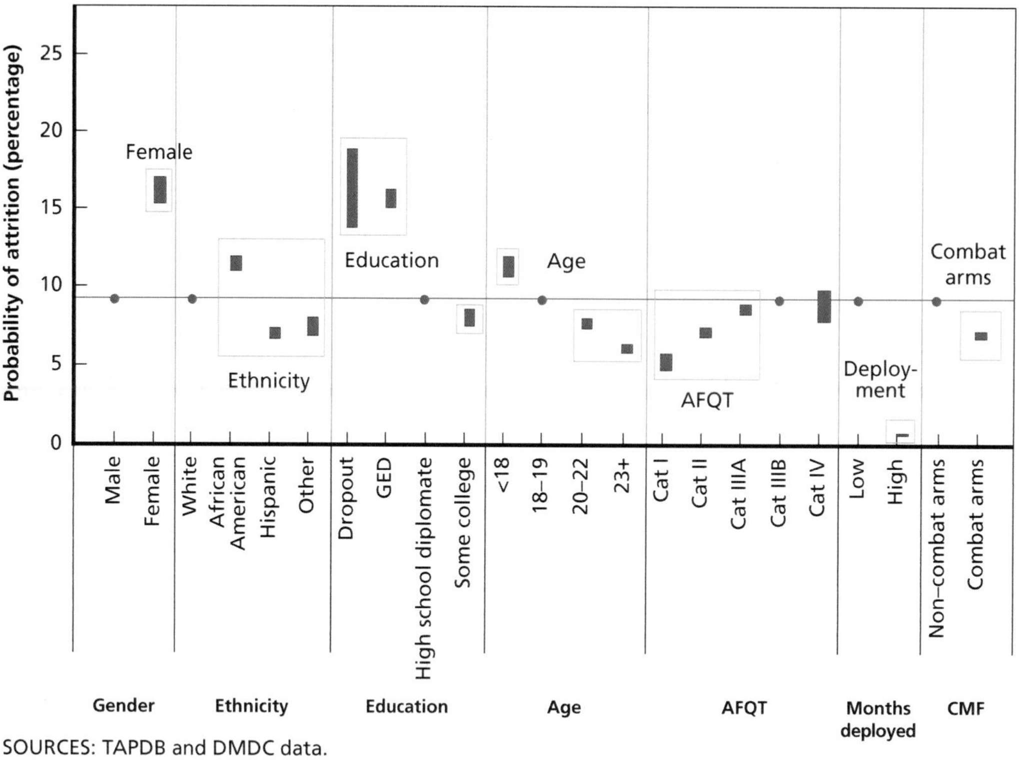

SOURCES: TAPDB and DMDC data.
NOTE: As is the case for all results reported, regression results hold constant other characteristics (institutional and leader, in this case).
RAND RR2211-A.1

well as the standard errors associated with the estimates (in square brackets). In each case, the outcome was modeled using a logit or logistic regression; regression models also included indicator variables for location at the largest bases, location at one of the smaller bases, FY, and quarter of enlistment.

Figures A.1–A.6 include marginal effects from the soldier and location variables included in the models discussed in this appendix (marginal effects of senior leaders' characteristics are presented in Chapter Three).

We also explored alternative measures of first-term soldiers' performance. In particular, we examined 48-month failure-to-adapt attrition, as well as 36- and 48-month continuation rates.

Continuation rate is defined as the percentage of soldiers remaining in the enlisted force at a certain time after their initial enlistment date. The continuation rate implicitly captures reenlistment because it generally occurs at a set time after initial enlistment; this is more relevant at the 48-month point than at the 36-month point. In

Figure A.2
Probability of 36-Month Attrition, by Installation

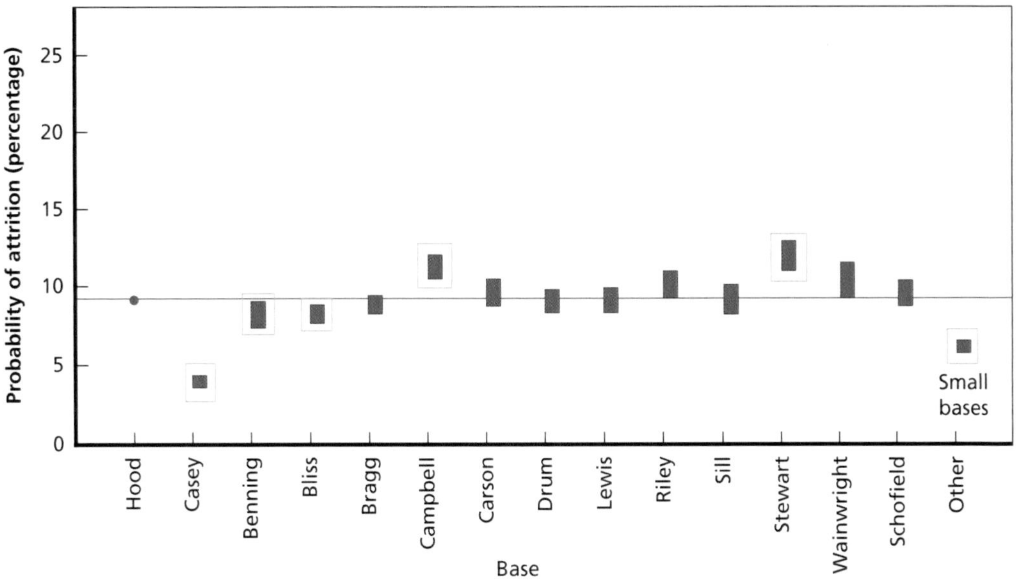

SOURCES: TAPDB and DMDC data.
RAND RR2211-A.2

general, continuation rates have remained fairly steady across the time period covered by our sample.

Table A.4 includes the results from these alternative outcomes. In general, the results are quite comparable to those shown in Table A.3—individual soldier characteristics dominate these results, but senior leader characteristics are important in some cases as well. Attrition is lower, and continuation is higher, in units with typical values for TIS and promotion speed to E-6.

Figure A.3
Probability of Early Promotion to E-5 as a Function of Soldier Characteristics

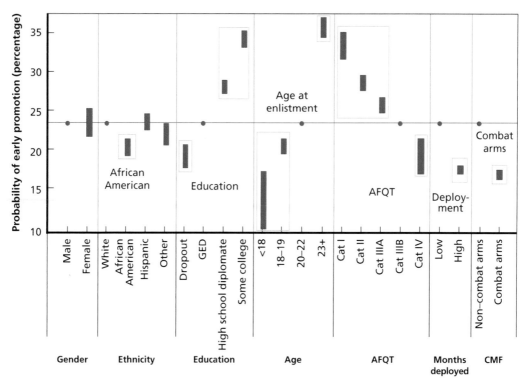

SOURCES: TAPDB and DMDC data.
RAND RR2211-A.3

Figure A.4
Probability of Early Promotion to E-5, by Installation

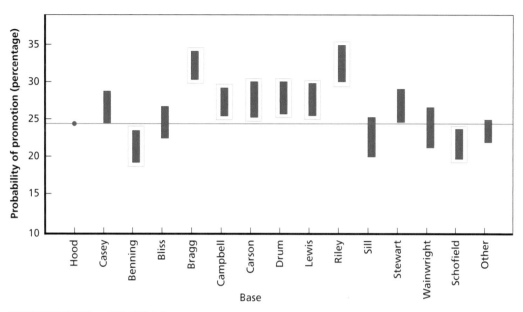

SOURCES: TAPDB and DMDC data.
RAND *RR2211-A.4*

Figure A.5
Probability of Demotion from E-5 as a Function of Soldier Characteristics

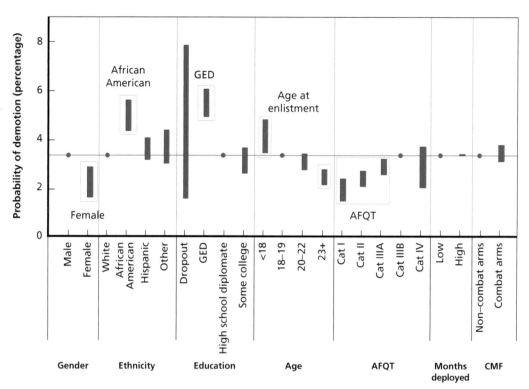

SOURCES: TAPDB and DMDC data.

Figure A.6
Probability of Demotion from E-5, by Installation

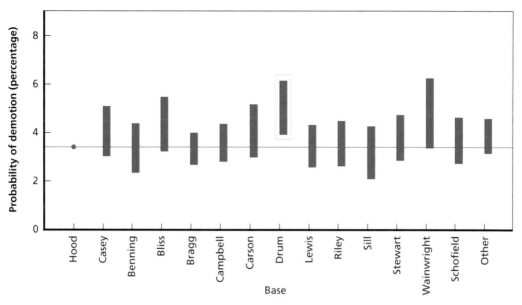

SOURCES: TAPDB and DMDC data.
RAND RR2211-A.6

Table A.4
Regression Results: Continuation and 48-Month Attrition

Variable	48-Month Failure-to-Adapt Attrition	36-Month Continuation	48-Month Continuation
Soldier characteristics			
Women	0.727***	−0.443***	−0.209***
	[0.665, 0.789]	[−0.498, −0.388]	[−0.263, −0.155]
African American	0.277***	−0.0817***	0.234***
	[0.229, 0.324]	[−0.122, −0.0410]	[0.196, 0.271]
Hispanic	−0.303***	0.167***	0.154***
	[−0.354, −0.252]	[0.126, 0.207]	[0.119, 0.190]
Other	−0.250***	0.148***	0.0926***
	[−0.326, −0.175]	[0.0883, 0.208]	[0.0410, 0.144]
<u>Age at enlistment</u>			
Younger than 18 years of age	0.230***	0.149***	−0.0058
	[0.168, 0.292]	[−0.205, −0.0942]	[−0.0575, 0.0459]

Table A.4—Continued

Variable	48-Month Failure-to-Adapt Attrition	36-Month Continuation	48-Month Continuation
20–22	−0.205***	0.0904***	0.0604***
	[−0.241, −0.169]	[0.0605, 0.120]	[0.0336, 0.0872]
23 years of age or older	−0.436***	0.173***	0.167***
	[−0.481, −0.390]	[0.137, 0.210]	[0.135, 0.199]
Education			
Dropout	0.679***	−0.441***	−0.378***
	[0.511, 0.848]	[−0.602, −0.281]	[−0.521, −0.234]
GED	0.603***	−0.445***	−0.387***
	[0.565, 0.641]	[−0.479, −0.411]	[−0.418, −0.356]
College or some college	−0.159***	−0.0164	−0.132***
	[−0.224, −0.0947]	[−0.0645, 0.0316]	[−0.174, −0.0904]
AFQT score			
AFQT cat I	−0.546***	0.309***	0.308***
	[−0.635, −0.457]	[0.244, 0.374]	[0.254, 0.363]
AFQT cat II	−0.223***	0.284***	0.399***
	[−0.262, −0.184]	[0.252, 0.316]	[0.371, 0.428]
AFQT cat IIIa	−0.0259	0.165***	0.354***
	[−0.0646, 0.0127]	[0.133, 0.198]	[0.324, 0.384]
AFQT cat IV	−0.0896	0.161***	0.157***
	[−0.196, 0.0173]	[0.0672, 0.254]	[0.0791, 0.236]
Non–combat arms	−0.138***	0.439***	0.239***
	[−0.172, −0.103]	[0.409, 0.468]	[0.214, 0.264]
Deployment experience			
Deployed	−2.410***	2.175***	2.123***
	[−2.458, −2.362]	[2.137, 2.213]	[2.093, 2.154]
Deployed by E-5	–	–	–
	–	–	–

Table A.4—Continued

Variable	48-Month Failure-to-Adapt Attrition	36-Month Continuation	48-Month Continuation
Leader characteristics			
<u>TIS</u>			
Less than 22 years	0.210***	−0.251***	−0.133***
	[0.169, 0.252]	[−0.285, −0.217]	[−0.164, −0.101]
25 or more years	0.0752***	−0.0495**	−0.0799***
	[0.0376, 0.113]	[−0.0808, −0.0182]	[−0.107, −0.0524]
Time in unit is less than 15 months	0.317***	−0.371***	−0.166***
	[0.283, 0.350]	[−0.399, −0.344]	[−0.192, −0.140]
<u>Promotion speed to E–6</u>			
Fastest to E-6	−0.0459	0.0146	−0.0573**
	[−0.0995, 0.00764]	[−0.0298, 0.0590]	[−0.0973, −0.0174]
Second quartile to E-6	−0.281***	0.224***	0.107***
	[−0.334, −0.228]	[0.180, 0.268]	[0.0677, 0.146]
Third quartile to E-6	−0.178***	0.234***	0.0908***
	[−0.251, −0.106]	[0.173, 0.294]	[0.0381, 0.143]
Fourth quartile to E-6	−0.0613*	0.0473	−0.00508
	[−0.122, −0.000406]	[−0.00332, 0.0978]	[−0.0506, 0.0405]
<u>AFQT score</u>			
AFQT cat I	−0.0742	−0.194***	−0.0224
	[−0.208, 0.0598]	[−0.307, −0.0802]	[−0.130, 0.0851]
AFQT cat II	−0.0231	0.0520**	0.0979***
	[−0.0625, 0.0164]	[0.0194, 0.0847]	[0.0685, 0.127]
AFQT cat IIIa	−0.151***	0.181***	0.167***
	[−0.191, −0.112]	[0.149, 0.214]	[0.138, 0.196]
AFQT cat IV	0.211***	−0.243***	−0.132***
	[0.152, 0.269]	[−0.292, −0.194]	[−0.178, −0.0872]
<u>Senior deployment experience</u>			
Not yet deployed	1.054***	−0.982***	−0.574***
	[0.973, 1.135]	[−1.052, −0.913]	[−0.639, −0.509]

Table A.4—Continued

Variable	48-Month Failure-to-Adapt Attrition	36-Month Continuation	48-Month Continuation
1–19 months	0.330***	−0.415***	−0.220***
	[0.289, 0.371]	[−0.451, −0.380]	[−0.251, −0.188]
More than 40 months	0.133**	−0.0960**	−0.0486
	[0.0505, 0.216]	[−0.158, −0.0339]	[−0.105, 0.00805]
Constant	−1.898***	0.752***	−0.462***
	[−2.006, −1.790]	[0.663, 0.841]	[−0.542, −0.381]
Pseudo R-squared	0.17	0.15	0.147

NOTE: Modeling promotion required a slightly different specification because the sample size was smaller. Stars indicate level of statistical significance: * 10 percent; ** 5 percent; *** 1 percent.

Noncommissioned Officer Education System Courses, 2001–2015

Purpose

We provide a brief examination of the Active Component NCO Education System (NCOES) courses, with particular attention to how the courses changed over the period of time covered by our data and how these changes might be expected to affect the productivity of NCOs.

Background

The NCOES is a major component of the Army's system for developing a professional and competent NCO corps; thus, a key characteristic of each NCO is the type and timing of NCOES training received.

The NCOES provides NCOs with progressive and sequential training related to the anticipated responsibilities and missions they will perform after graduation.[1] The training and education process for the NCO begins with a leadership development course that is standard for all NCOs, regardless of branch. The second course is branch-specific, as is the third; the final culminating course is branch-immaterial. Specifically, the courses currently include the following:

- *Warrior Leader Course (WLC)*, previously known as the Primary Leader Development Course (PLDC). This four-week-long course provides basic training on leader skills, as well as the knowledge and information needed to lead team- and squad-sized units.
- *Advanced Leader Course (ALC)*, previously known as Basic NCO Course (BNCOC) (Department of the Army, 2001b). Up to eight weeks long, this

---

[1] The material in this section is drawn from NCOES, 2012.

branch-specific course provides soldiers who have been selected for promotion to E-6 with exposure to relevant leader, technical, and tactical skills and knowledge needed to lead squad- and platoon-sized units.

- **Senior Leader Course (SLC)**, previously known as Advanced NCO Course (ANCOC) (Department of the Army, 2000). Up to eight weeks long, this branch-specific course provides soldiers selected for promotion to E-7 with exposure to relevant leader, technical, and tactical skills and knowledge needed to perform as senior NCOs in platoon- and company-sized units.
- **Sergeants Major Course (SMC)**: The capstone course is designed for the master sergeant (MSG), MSG (promotable), sergeant major, and CSM and serves to prepare them for higher-level troop and staff assignments, specifically at the battalion and brigade levels. This course focuses on a variety of aspects of leadership, with specific emphasis on combat and sustainment operations, team building, communication skills, training management, and professional development.

Except for the SMC, NCOs normally attend these courses "on unit time"; that is, the NCO goes to the course while assigned to a position in a unit. Therefore, the unit does not have a leader in the position during the time that the NCO is taking the course. Given this potential impact on unit functioning and training, the amount of time that Army policy leaders have allocated to course attendance has been relatively limited compared with the amount of time allocated for officers. Officers generally attend longer professional development courses on a permanent-change-of-station basis, which does not cause a unit position to be vacant.

- **Structured Self-Development (SSD)** is also considered a part of NCOES. It consists of online, self-paced lessons that the soldier must take as a prerequisite to attending a resident NCOES course. There are five levels of SSD: SSD I is a prerequisite for WLC, SSD II is a prerequisite for ALC, SSD III is a prerequisite for SLC, SSD IV is a prerequisite for SMC, and SSD V is a prerequisite for nominative assignments. Each level has been developed to take about 80 hours to complete. Prior to the implementation of SSD, BNCOC and ANCOC had a branch-immaterial common core (CC) phase.

Research Approach

We first did an overall examination of the NCOES. Because the larger research effort examined the relationship between NCO experience and productivity for the full range of NCO grades and at higher grades, the NCO would have attended several NCOES courses. We examined not only current courses but also the earlier courses that current NCOs would have attended.

We then selected a set of courses to examine in depth, made contact with proponent staff for each, and asked them to provide three Programs of Instruction (POIs) for these courses across the period since deployments began (2002, currently taught, and a midpoint). We then examined these POIs and, based on the overall and specific NCOES course examination, concluded that (1) the degree to which the NCOES generally and each specifically would improve NCO productivity and (2) the degree to which this relationship changed across the period examined.

We then vetted our findings and conclusions with a range of Army experts and revised them as appropriate.

Courses Selected

We selected a sufficient number of courses to provide a reasonable basis for arriving at conclusions on the benefit to NCO productivity. The courses selected were as follows:

- WLC was selected because it is the fundamental course supporting the transition from soldier follower to NCO leader, and it is taught to all junior NCOs.
- The CC/SSD courses were selected because they are taught to all NCOs as they progress in grade and because the ability of NCOs to develop their subordinates is a skill likely to be included in these common courses.
- ALC and SLC for infantrymen (11B) and cannon crewmen (13B) were selected because there are a large number of NCOs in these MOSs and the combat arms focus is appropriate given that the data set used in our primary analyses focuses on soldiers who are assigned to MTOE units.

Levels of Productivity

We examined the courses to look at three levels of productivity:

- *Overall NCO productivity* applies to the broad aspect of benefit to the Army. The ability of the Army to function on a day-to-day basis and perform in operational missions is directly related to NCO productivity. Benefits include not only success in general leadership and supervision functions but also small-unit tactical success. This is why the NCO corps is called the Army's "backbone."
- *Developing subordinates generally* applies to the benefits of the graduate's ability to develop subordinates.
- *Impact on developing subordinates in the specific measures being analyzed in the broader research effort* applies to the benefits of the graduate's ability to develop their subordinates in a way that affects the subordinates' promotion rates and timing, lack of demotions, and retention.

Changes in the NCOES, 2002–2015

In 2002, NCOES courses were designed to teach the critical MOS-specific and general leadership skills needed to perform at the next-higher grade. NCOs were required to complete the needed course prior to promotion (i.e., a process model of select-train-promote). Descriptions of the NCOES courses in 2002 are as follows:

- WLC, then known as the PLDC, was a 28-day residential course that taught general leadership skills and required common subjects/skills needed to serve as a sergeant E-5 team-level leader. It was designed to transition the soldier from being a follower to being an NCO leader. It had no MOS-specific tasks, and all soldiers attended the same course.
- ALC, then known as BNCOC, consisted of two phased residential courses, generally eight- to 12-week-long phases. The first phase was CC, which taught general leadership skills and selected required common subjects/skills. The second phase taught MOS-specific critical tasks/skills needed to serve as a staff sergeant (SSG) E-6 squad-/section-level leader.
- SLC, then known as ANCOC, also consisted of two phased courses, generally eight to 12 weeks long. The first phase, CC, taught general leadership skills and selected required common subjects/skills, and MOS-specific critical tasks/skills needed to serve as a sergeant first class (SFC) E-7 platoon sergeant–level leader were taught in the second phase.

In 2002, completion of these courses was linked to promotion. Some "conditional" promotions were authorized, but PLDC was a requirement for permanent promotion to sergeant E-5, BNCOC was a requirement for permanent promotion to SSG E-6, and ANCOC was a requirement for permanent promotion to SFCs E-7.

Starting in 2002, the large-scale operational deployments to Iraq and Afghanistan disrupted timely attendance at NCOES courses, especially for NCOs in the combat arms MOSs. Unit deployments were frequent, and time between deployments was limited. During the period between deployments, the highest priorities were unit training and preparation for the next deployment, as well as giving soldiers time to recover and reunite with their families. Therefore, many NCOs were not able to attend NCOES courses on timelines that supported effective professional development.

As it became apparent that requiring completion of the NCOES for promotion was neither practical nor fair to soldiers or to units training for deployment, the Army backed off the requirement for NCOES attendance prior to promotion and increasingly allowed "conditional" promotions where the NCO could be promoted before attending the required courses. This resulted in a large backlog of NCOs who did not attend required courses until well after promotion and after serving in the positions the courses were designed to teach. This in turn reduced the relevance of the courses for many who did attend because they had served years in the positions the courses were designed to train, and, in some cases, they were actually performing in higher positions at the time of attending the course. In some cases, such a training requirement "after the fact" could even have had a negative effect on morale, leader effectiveness, or both (to our knowledge, there is no research examining this question).

In January 2004, the policies changed in response to these circumstances. Conditional promotions were no longer authorized, but the link to promotions was shifted up one level or "to the right." Thus, there was no NCOES requirement for promotion to sergeant E-5; rather, PLDC was made a requirement for promotion to SSG E-6, BNCOC for promotion to SFC E-7, and ANCOC for promotion to MSG E-8. This shift greatly reduced the required amount of formal NCOES training received across all grades (Tice, 2015). For example, in 2004, ANCOC would have been required for promotion to SFC (then at about 14 YOSs), but, with the changed policy, the equivalent SLC was required for promotion to MSG, which occurred at about 17.5 YOSs. Moreover, even after this loosening of promotion requirements, there were still periods when limited conditional promotions were permitted for deployed soldiers under the new promotion requirements.[2]

In 2004, the Commander of TRADOC directed the implementation of a *NCOES Transformation* (Combined Arms Center, Headquarters, 2005). As a part of this program, the names of the PLDC, BNCOC, and ANCOC were changed to WLC, ALC and SLC. In addition, over the subsequent few years, more changes were made to decrease the difficulties of attending, and still other changes were made to increase the relevance of the courses. Examples of these changes include the following:

- Reduced course lengths. WLC was reduced to 15 days (from four weeks), and ALC and SLC to a maximum of eight weeks and often less (some were originally up to 12 weeks long) (Combined Arms Center, 2005).
- Developed a series of online 80-hour asynchronous SSD courses (termed SSD I, III, and IV) and a synchronous video teletraining (VTT) ALC CC course to teach required CC subjects and to support reduced course length by the elimination of CC in resident training. However, the development was slow, and SSD I (WLC), III (SLC), and IV (SMC) were made requirements for NCOES attendance and graduation effective only in April 2013 for WLC and in June 2013 for SLC (HQDA, 2012b). ALC CC (which replaced the BNCOC and ANCOC CC) was a formal requirement for ALC graduation beginning in 2009, but many NCOs were promoted without meeting this requirement (HQDA, 2009).
- Began teaching selected courses at unit home station with Mobile Training Teams.

To make the courses more relevant, the changes included the following:

---

[2] The Army is planning to move back the NCOES requirement for promotion to the left in 2016; this change means that graduation from WLC (which will be renamed Basic Leader Course) will be a requirement for promotion to sergeant E-5.

- WLC, ALC, and SLC were redesigned to include next-higher grade skills and tasks. For example, ALCs were to be designed to teach platoon- and squad-level tasks and skills.
- Critical tasks required for performance during operational deployment (e.g., lessons learned, reaction to improvised explosive devices) or postdeployment (suicide prevention) were added.

The combination of lessened NCOES requirements for promotion and shortened courses resulted in a significant reduction in time spent in required NCOES training. For example, in 2002, a typical SFC would have had about 24 weeks of NCOES training (four weeks of PLDC, ten weeks of BNCOC, and ten weeks of ANCOC). In contrast, after NCOES transformation and changes to the NCOES promotion requirements, the length of time a typical SFC devoted to NCOES training would have been cut by more than one-half, to about ten weeks (two weeks of WLC and eight weeks of ALC).

In addition to a reduction in the total time devoted to NCOES training, changes in the emphasis of course content likely had the effect of further reducing the training on subordinate development skills in the NCOES. The lessened emphasis on leadership skills was furthered by the elimination of CC training requirements (until 2014, when SSD completion was required for NCOES course attendance). In the next section, we discuss the course changes in more detail.

Examination of Selected Courses

We examined the selected courses in the areas of purpose, length, content, and the training devoted directly to improving the NCO's ability to develop subordinates. The results of this examination are outlined in Tables B.1–B.8 and accompanying explanations.

Table B.1
Basic Non-Commissioned Officer Course and Advanced Non-Commissioned Officer Course Common Core in 2002

	BNCOC CC[a]	ANCOC CC[b]
Purpose	To prepare SSGs and selected promotable sergeants to perform the duties and execute the responsibilities of NCOs To use the small-group instruction process to teach the theory and principles of battle-focused CC training and warfighting skills required to lead a squad-/section-size element in combat	To prepare SFCs and selected promotable sergeants to perform the duties and execute the responsibilities of senior NCOs; to teach the theory and principles of battle focused CC training, and the warfighting skills required to lead a platoon-size element in combat
Length	2 weeks 2 days (12 instructional days)	2 weeks 2 days (12 instructional days)
Academic/administrative hours	74/0 hours	77.5/0 hours
Content summary/key points	• Leadership skills (18 hours) • Communication skills (10 hours) • Professional skills (5 hours) • Training skills (16 hours) • Warfighting skills (15 hours)	• Leadership skills (21 hours) • Communication skills (9 hours) • Professional skills (4 hours) • Resourcing skills (9.5 hours) • Health skills (2 hours) • Training skills (16 hours) • Warfighting skills (6 hours)
Direct "developing" subordinates training	• Motivate subordinates to improve performance (3 hours) • Counsel subordinates (5 hours) • Develop subordinates in squads (5 hours) • NCOER rater responsibilities (2 hours)	• Motivate subordinates to accomplish mission (3 hours) • Counsel subordinates (5 hours) • Develop subordinate leaders in platoon (5 hours)

[a] Department of the Army, 2001b.

[b] Department of the Army, 2000.

These courses provided some general leadership lessons, including some that would directly enhance developing subordinate skills.

Table B.2
Advanced Leader Course After Noncommissioned Officer Transformation

Aspect of Course	ALC CC 2009
Purpose	To provide all sergeants and SSGs with the latest leadership technical and tactical values, attributes, skills, and actions needed to lead a squad or platoon to accomplish a mission
Length	N/A
Academic/administrative hours	80.4/52
Content summary/key points	This is an online facilitated (instructor–student interaction) asynchronous course taught in a 90-day period. The course has leadership, training, and warfighting lessons. Most leadership lessons are listed below.
Direct developing-subordinates training	• NCO evaluation reporting (3 hours) • Identify the warning signs of a potential suicide (2 hours) • Implement measures to reduce combat stress in a squad/section (3 hours) • Implement measures to reduce combat stress in a squad/section (3 hours)

SOURCE: Department of the Army, 2009a.

The initial SSD I, III, and IV courses are not shown because the information could not be located during our research effort. It was apparently lost during a transition to a new data system.

The ALC CC contains leader and developing subordinates' skills but less than the BNCOC and ANCOC CC courses replaced. Moreover, the consideration that these are done in an extended online mode and not in a full-time residence means that the development of subordinates and general productivity benefit would be less. Additionally, the fact that these were not made direct NCOES requirements until 2014 meant that the benefit of these courses would have to be considered low.

Table B.3
Structured Self-Development I–IV 2014

Aspect of Course	SSD I	SSD II	SSD III	SSD IV
Requirement for attendance at	WLC	ALC	SLC	SMC
Length, in hours	80	80	80	80
Total lessons	32	34	25	14
General leadership	8	5	12	0
General NCO knowledge/skills	15	2	5	6
Warfighting	8	25	7	7
Directly related to developing subordinates	• Identify the impacts of war and multiple deployments on subordinates	• Prepare a NCO evaluation report • Supervise the Army's sexual assault prevention and response program (intermediate leader)	• Develop a company mentorship program	• Develop a mentorship program at battalion and higher levels

As with BNCOC and ANCOC CC, these 80-hour courses include some general leadership lessons, as those would directly enhance developing subordinate skills. But these were self-paced online courses and were not mandatory until 2014; thus, there would likely be considerably less learning than implied by the number of lessons listed.

Table B.4
Primary Leader Development Course/Warrior Leader Course

Aspect of Course	PLDC 2001	WLC 2007	WLC 2015
Purpose	To prepare selected promotable specialists/ corporals, and sergeants to perform the duties and execute the responsibilities of junior NCOs and to teach them how to train and lead the soldiers who will work and fight under their supervision	To prepare selected SSGs; promotable specialists/ corporals, and sergeants; specialist/corporals nonpromotable; and privates first class in the priority outlined in AR 350-1	To prepare selected SSGs, sergeants, promotable specialist/corporals, and nonpromotable specialists and corporals who can visualize, describe, and execute squad-level operations in varied operational environments and are predictive, adaptive, and innovative combat leaders
Length	4 weeks, 2 days (no weekend classes)	2 weeks, 1 day (15 days with weekend classes)	4 weeks (22 days)
Academic/ administrative hours	256.5/30 (includes 107 hours of individual self-study training)	199.6/37 Training on weekends and longer days	169/12 No weekend training and normal training days
Content summary/key points	The course focuses on leadership, general leader skills, and warfighter tasks and skills and includes • Leadership (32 hours) • Professional skills (e.g., conduct an inspection, wear of uniform) (42 hours) • Warfighter (e.g., combat orders, marksmanship) (38 hours, plus a 91-hour situational training exercise)	The course has increased focused on squad-level operations and training and somewhat less on leadership and general leader skills and includes • Leadership (24 hours) • Training (26 hours) • Warfighter (142 hours, including 96-hour situational training exercise)	The course remains focused on squad operations and training but has increased focus on leadership and includes • Leadership (41 hours) • Training (49 hours) • Squad operations (79 hours, including 36-hour situational training exercise)
Direct developing-subordinates training	• Conduct developmental counseling (2.6 hours) • Soldier team development (2 hours)	• Leadership (10 hours) • Conduct developmental counseling (5 hours) • NCO efficiency report (4 hours) • Sexual assault prevention and response training (2 hours)	• Leadership (7 hours) • Conduct developmental counseling (7 hours) • NCO efficiency report (5 hours) • Resilience (3 hours) • Sexual assault prevention and response training (3 hours) • Ethical problem solving (3 hours) • Military justice and discipline (2 hours) • Conduct individual training (5 hours)

[a] Department of the Army, 2001a.

[b] *Warrior Leader Course (MOD) 600-WLC Program of Instruction*, 2006.

[c] *Warrior Leader Course Program of Instruction*, July 2014.

This course is short, but a large portion of it is devoted, directly or indirectly, to developing subordinates. The 2007 reduction in course length lessened the benefit to some degree.

Table B.5
11B Basic Noncommissioned Officer Course/Advanced Leader Course

Aspect of Course	2002 11B BNCOC[a]	2009 11B ALC[b]	2014 11B ALC[c]
Purpose	To train infantry squad leaders to lead, train, and direct subordinates to maintain, operate, and employ weapons and equipment	Provides leader, technical, and tactical training relevant to duties, responsibilities, and missions faced in operational units	Train and educate infantry and NCOs to be adaptive leaders and critical and creative thinkers, with technical, tactical, administrative, and logistical skills to serve at squad and platoon levels
Length	5 weeks 2 days	4 weeks 3 days	5 weeks
Academic/administrative hours	277/26	206.3/36	248/22
Content summary/key points	Focus on squad-level tactical training and weapon training • No leadership hours in BNCOC CC • 122-hour field situational training exercise • Other training (e.g., swimming and land navigation)	Still focus on tactics and weapon training but tactics at platoon and squad levels and more focus on broader tactical concepts content • Only leadership lesson is mentoring • No field situational training exercise • 40 hour of combatives • Force XXI Battle Command Brigade and Below use in units and battle staff	Still focus on tactics and weapon training, but tactics at platoon and squad levels • 72-hour machine gun situational training exercise added • More live-weapon training • Combatives dropped • Tactical training included more-complex conditions
Direct developing-subordinates training	None, but again some in the phase 1 BNCOC CC	• Mentoring (8 hours)	• Promotion, separations, and Uniform Code of Military Justice (4 hours) • Resilience training for developing, mentoring, and ensuring mental health of subordinates (2 hours) • Effects of sexual harassment (2 hours)

[a] Department of the Army, 2001c.

[b] Department of the Army, 2009b.

[c] Department of the Army, 2014e.

In 2008, the course shifted to include a platoon as well as squad focus. It contained almost no direct general leadership or developing-subordinates training until 2014, when a small portion of the course was devoted to this area. However, the BNCOC and ALC CC provided benefit in this area.

Table B.6
11B Advanced Non-Commissioned Officer Course/Senior Leader Course

Aspect of Course	2002 11B ANCOC[a]	2010 11B SLC[b]	2015 11B SLC[c]
Purpose	Provide technical and tactical training to produce a more diverse small-unit leader; develops skills, knowledge, and behaviors to perform as platoon-level leader	Educate infantry and armor NCOs to be adaptive leaders and critical and creative thinkers, with technical, tactical, administrative, and logistical skills to serve at platoon and company levels and understanding of duties of a 1SG and battle staff NCO	Educate infantry and armor NCOs to be adaptive leaders and critical and creative thinkers, with technical, tactical, administrative, and logistical skills to serve at platoon and company levels and understanding of duties of a 1SG and battle staff NCO
Length days	8 weeks 2 days	7 weeks in 2 phases • Phase 1: maneuver SLC common (7 weeks) • Phase 2: 11B SLC (2 weeks)	7 weeks
Academic/ administrative hours	315.5/27	282.3/57 • Phase 1: 197.3/36 • Phase 2: 85/21	287.4/27

Content summary/ key points	General tactical doctrine with a focus on platoon-level tactics
	
	• No general leadership or developing-subordinates lessons in phase 2. See BNCOC phase 1 CC
	• Common training (119 hours)
	• Infantry tactical/technical training (196.5 hours)
	• Includes 72 hours field training exercise and 8 hours tactical exercise without troops in field
	• Other lessons/exercises:
	  ◦ Maintenance and logistics
	  ◦ Training management
	  ◦ Effective writing and basic computer
	  ◦ Land navigation and swimming
		Still a focus on platoon-level tactical skills, but some leadership/developing skills added
		
		• No CC or SSD III to supplement this
		• Lessons on company-level tactics and battle staff added
		• More-general tactical doctrine
		• No field training exercise, but 24-hour Close Combat Tactical Trainer and sergeant's training time
		• Increase company-level training management and garrison function lessons (e.g., drill and ceremony)
			Still focus on platoon tactical skills but compared with 2010
			
			• More-general subjects
			• Updated to current operational requirements (e.g., improvised explosive devices and situational awareness)
			• More time to company and battle staff skills
			• More time to garrison functions

Table B.6—Continued

Aspect of Course	2002 11B ANCOC[a]	2010 11B SLC[b]	2015 11B SLC[c]
Direct leader development lessons	None; see BNCOC phase 1 C	• Professional development counseling (11 hours) • Training and leader development, professional development, and mentoring (2 hours) • Problem solving, some involving leadership problems (4.6 hours) • Promotions, reductions, separations, Uniform Code of Military Justice, and absence without leave (8 hours)	Similar to 2010 with some additions (e.g., sexual harassment/assault response lesson added)

[a] Department of the Army, 2002a.

[b] Department of the Army, 2009c.

[c] Department of the Army, 2014c.

This course has focused mainly on infantry tactical and technical tasks/skills throughout the period. In 2002, there were no leadership lessons, but, in 2010, some leadership lessons were added. Additionally, in 2010, the course shifted to include a company as well as platoon focus.

Table B.7
13B Basic Non-Commissioned Officer Course/Advanced Leader Course

Year	2002 13B BNCOC[a]	2008 13B ALC[b]	2015 13B ALC[c]
Purpose	To train field artillery cannon section chiefs to lead, train, and direct subordinates to maintain, operate, and employ weapons and equipment	Same	Same
Length	2 weeks 3 days	5 weeks	5 weeks
Academic/ administrative hours	142/10	209/16	245/61.5 (includes physical training)
Content summary/key points	Course focuses almost exclusively on technical firing and equipment/ maintenance tasks and some tactics; 72-hour situational training exercise	Same	Same
Direct developing-subordinates training	None; see BNCOC phase 1 CC	• Leader development and decisionmaking (4 hours) • Army's sexual assault prevention and response training (3.9 hours)	• Resilience training (1 hour) • Army's sexual assault prevention and response training (1 hour) • Leader development and decisionmaking (1 hour)

[a] Department of the Army, 2002b.

[b] Department of the Army, 2007. Note that we chose this rather than a later ALC version because it represents a closer to midpoint course and was fielded well after the initiation of the NCOES Transformation initiative.

[c] Department of the Army, 2014a.

This course focused almost exclusively on FA technical and tactical tasks and skills throughout period. It more than doubled in 2008 as extended deployments with most FA soldiers performing non-FA missions generated a need to enhance FA training. The 2008 and 2015 versions had some leadership lessons but far fewer than in ANCOC CC.

Table B.8
13B Advanced Non-Commissioned Officer Course/Senior Leader Course

Year	2002 13B ANCOC[a]	2008 13B SLC[b]	2015 13B SLC[c]
Purpose	To teach the 13B40 to perform skill level 4 tasks focused on the duties of the platoon sergeant, chief of firing battery, gunnery sergeant, battalion master gunner, and the battalion ammunition NCO	To train the cannon senior NCOs to perform the duties of the rank SFC to include platoon sergeant, chief of firing battery, gunnery sergeant, battalion master gunner, battalion ammunition NCO, as well as assume the duties of the 1SG and executive officer or platoon leader in their absence	Same
Length	3 weeks 4 days	6 weeks 4 days	6 weeks 3 days
Academic/administrative hours	178/23	277.1/32	287.8/63.5 (includes 26 hours physical training)
Content summary/key points	Course focuses almost exclusively on technical firing and equipment/maintenance tasks and some tactics; 72-hour situational training exercise See ANCOC Phase 1 CC	Course focuses heavily on technical firing and equipment/maintenance tasks and some tactics • Still an almost exclusive focus on FA SFC E-7 tasks and skills • 72-hour situational training exercise	Same
Direct developing-subordinates training	None, see ANCOC phase 1 CC	• NCODP (2 hours) • Ethics/leader decision process (4 hours) • Soldiers (1 hour) • NCOER (3 hours) • Awards and decorations (1 hour) • Manage promotions and reductions (2 hours) • Maintain a weight-control program (2 hours) • Training management (4 hours) • Role of 1SG (3 hours)	Similar to 2008 with some additions • Sexual harassment/assault response program (1.2 hours)

[a] Department of the Army, 2001d.

[b] Department of the Army, 2008.

[c] Department of the Army, 2014d.

This course focused almost exclusively on FA technical and tactical tasks and skills in 2002; in 2008, the focus remained the same, but the course nearly doubled in length as extended deployments with most FA soldiers performing non-FA missions generated a need to enhance FA training. The 2008 and 2015 versions had some leadership lessons but far less than in the ANCOC CC.

In most cases, the examination of specific courses aligns to the general observations on NCOES benefit to productivity and how this changed between 2002 and today. The 13B courses were an exception in that overall course length increased as opposed to decreasing, but, as explained above, this represented a special case and did not lead to more training with regard to developing subordinates. In fact, given the elimination of residential BNCOC and ANCOC CC with no required replacement until SSD was made an NCOES attendance requirement, the developing-subordinate undoubtedly lessened.

Conclusions

We draw the following conclusions based on the overall and specific course examination of NCOES:

- Compared with operational experience, the impact of NCOES on NCO productivity is likely to be important but small.

There is an Army-wide consensus that NCOES plays a critical role in developing the professionalism of the NCOES Corps. However, the amount of time spent in these courses is relatively small. A typical current NCO would have attended the three courses for a total of five to seven months over an 11- to 15-year period, and many of today's NCOs would have attended courses later than would be desirable to gain the full benefit.

- The emphasis on the NCOs' ability to develop subordinates is even smaller, but nonetheless is still considered important.

Only WLC/PLDC have had a major focus on leadership skills, and, even in this course, only a small amount of time is devoted to teaching NCOs the skills that directly relate to developing their subordinates. The percentage of time in other NCOES courses directly related to the development of subordinates' skills is much smaller and, for some courses during the period, was almost nonexistent.

- There would likely be very little NCOES impact on our specific productivity measures.

The amount of time in NCOES courses devoted to developing subordinates' skills is small, and there is no reason to think that this small amount of time would have any real impact on our specific productivity measures.

Because few of the senior leaders had taken the updated courses described here, we could not estimate the direct effect of changes to NCOES on the productivity of senior NCOs in our sample. However, the analysis here suggests that such effects would likely be minimal, especially when compared with other aspects of experience (such as deployment experience, TIS, or TIG).

Interview Protocol

The purpose of this interview is to understand your experiences with leaders in the Army. When we ask you about your experiences, please do not use the names of your leaders or other personnel. You can refer to the leader as "he" or "she" or, if you prefer, make up a name for that person.

First, I would like to get some background information about you.

1. What is your rank? _____

2. When did you enlist in the Army? Month _____ Year _____

3. Have you been deployed? Yes _____   No _____

4. If yes, where have you been deployed and how long was each deployment?
    a. Location _____   Duration _____
    b. Location _____   Duration _____
    c. Location _____   Duration _____
    d. Location _____   Duration _____

5. What is your career management field (CMF)? _____

6. Think about an NCO leader that you have had in the Army who motivated you to do your best work.

    a. What did this leader do that was particularly effective?

    b. Can you think of a specific situation in which this leader demonstrated _____ [response(s) from 6a]

        i.   What was the situation?
        ii. What did he or she do?

       iii.   What happened as a result?

    c.   How long did you work with this leader?

    d.   What was this leader's rank when you worked with him/her?

    e.   When did this leader enter the Army?

    f.   Had this leader been deployed at the time that you worked with him/her or before that time? If so, how many deployments and where was he or she deployed?

7.   Think about an NCO leader that you have had in the Army who did not motivate you to do your best work.

    a.   What did this leader do that was particularly ineffective?

    b.   Can you think of a specific situation in which this leader demonstrated _____[response from 7a]

       i.   What was the situation?
       ii.   What did he or she do?
       iii.   What happened as a result?

    c.   How long did you work with this leader?

    d.   What was this leader's rank when you worked with him/her?

    e.   When did this leader enter the Army?

    f.   Had this leader been deployed at the time that you worked with him/her or before that time? If so, how many deployments and where was he or she deployed?

8.   How did your experiences with NCO leadership affect you? For example, your decision to reenlist your access to opportunities, or how well you performed your duties and responsibilities?

9.   Who do you seek out for career advice? Such advice could include specific information about how to get promoted, as well as options about reenlistment, mentorship, etc.?

10. Finally, is there anything that you want to add about your experience with particularly effective or ineffective leaders in the Army?

Thank you for sharing your views and for your time.

References

Asch, Beth J., John A. Romley, and Mark E. Totten, *The Quality of Personnel in the Enlisted Ranks*, Santa Monica, Calif.: RAND Corporation, MG-324-OSD, 2005. As of March 9, 2018: https://www.rand.org/pubs/monographs/MG324.html

Atwater, Leanne E., Shelley D. Dionne, Bruce Avolio, John F. Camobreco, and Alan W. Lau, "A Longitudinal Study of the Leadership Development Process: Individual Differences Predicting Leader Effectiveness," *Human Relations*, Vol. 52, No. 12, December 1999, pp. 1543–1562.

Bass, Bernard M., "From Transactional to Transformational Leadership: Learning to Share the Vision," *Organizational Dynamics*, Vol. 18, No. 3, Winter 1990, pp. 19–31.

Borman, Walter C., and Stephan J. Motowidlo, "Task Performance and Contextual Performance: The Meaning for Personnel Selection Research," *Human Performance*, Vol. 10, No. 2, 1997, pp. 99–109.

Boyd, Donald, Pam Grossman, Marsha Ing, Hamilton Lankford, Susanna Loeb, and James Wyckoff, "The Influence of School Administrators on Teacher Retention Decisions," *American Educational Research Journal*, Vol. 48, No. 2, April 2011, pp. 303–333.

Boyle, Diane K., Marjorie J. Bott, Helen E. Hansen, Cynthia Q. Woods, and Roma Lee Taunton, "Manager's Leadership and Critical Care Nurses' Intent to Stay," *American Journal of Critical Care*, Vol. 8, No. 6, 1999, p. 361–371.

Buddin, Richard, *Success of First-Term Soldiers: The Effects of Recruiting Practices and Recruit Characteristics*, Santa Monica, Calif.: RAND Corporation, MG-262-A, 2005. As of March 11, 2018: https://www.rand.org/pubs/monographs/MG262.html

Clotfelter, Charles T., Helen F. Ladd, and Jacob L. Vigno, "Teacher Credentials and Student Achievement: Longitudinal Analysis with Student Fixed Effects," *Economics of Education Review*, Vol. 26, No. 6, December 2007, pp. 673–682.

Combined Arms Center, Headquarters, *NCOES Transformation*, Operations Order 05-165A, July 25, 2005.

Conway, James M., "Distinguishing Contextual Performance from Task Performance for Managerial Jobs," *Journal of Applied Psychology*, Vol. 84, No. 1, 1999, pp. 3–13.

Dentsen, Iain L., "Senior Police Leadership: Does Rank Matter?" *Policing*, Vol. 26, No. 3, September 2003, pp. 400–418.

Department of the Army, *Advanced Noncommissioned Officer Course (Common Core): The Army Training System (TATS)*, October 2000.

Department of the Army, *The Army Training System Primary Leadership Course POI*, April 2001a.

Department of the Army, *Basic Noncommissioned Officer Course (Stand Alone Common Core)*, 600-00-BNCOC, June 2001b.

Department of the Army, *Program of Instruction, Infantryman BNCOC*, June 2001c.

Department of the Army, *Program of Instruction TATS Field Artillery Platoon Sergeant, ANCOC*, December 2001d.

Department of the Army, *Infantryman ANCOC Phase 2 POI*, January 2002a.

Department of the Army, *Program of Instruction TATS Field Artillery Cannon Section Chief, BNCOC*, October 2002b.

Department of the Army, *NCOES Transformation Headquarters Combined Arms Center*, Operations Order 05-165A, July 25, 2005.

Department of the Army, *Program of Instruction Field Artillery Cannon Section Chief, BNCOC*, June 2007.

Department of the Army, *Program of Instruction, FA Platoon Sergeant, SLC*, July 2008.

Department of the Army, *Program of Instruction Advanced Leader–Common Core*, January 2009a.

Department of the Army, *Program of Instruction (POI) for Advanced Leader Course (ALC)*, February 2009b.

Department of the Army, *Maneuver SLC POI*, April 2009c.

Department of the Army, *Program of Instruction Field Artillery Cannon Section Chief, ALC*, May 2014a.

Department of the Army, "The U.S. Army Human Dimension Concept," TRADOC Pam 525-3-7, May 21, 2014b. As of September 18, 2015:
http://www.tradoc.army.mil/tpubs/pams/TP525-3-7.pdf

Department of the Army, *Maneuver SLC POI*, June 2014c.

Department of the Army, *Program of Instruction, FA Platoon Sergeant, SLC*, June 2014d.

Department of the Army, *Program of Instruction (POI) for 010-11B30-C45, Infantryman ALC*, July 2014e.

Dvir, Taly, Dov Eden, Bruce J. Avolio, and Boas Shamir, "Impact of Transformational Leadership on Follower Development and Performance: A Field Experiment," *Academy of Management Journal*, Vol. 45, No. 4, August 2002, pp. 735–744.

Eisenberger, Robert, Florence Stinglhamber, Christian Vandenberghe, Ivan L. Sucharski, and Linda Rhoades, "Perceived Supervisor Support: Contributions to Perceived Organizational Support and Employee Retention," *Journal of Applied Psychology*, Vol. 87, No. 3, 2002, p. 565–573.

Fiedler, Fred E., "Research on Leadership Selection and Training: One View of the Future," *Administrative Science Quarterly*, Vol. 41, No. 2, June 1996, pp. 241–250.

Headquarters, Department of the Army, *Military Justice*, Washington, D.C., Army Regulation 27-10, June 24, 1996.

Headquarters, Department of the Army, *Subject ALARACT 262/2009: Implementation of Advanced Leader Course*, All Army Activity 262/2009, September 2009.

Headquarters, Department of the Army, *Army Leadership*, Washington, D.C., Army Doctrine Reference Publication 6-22, August 2012a.

Headquarters, Department of the Army, *Structured Self-Development (SSD) Governance: Implementation of SSD Policy*, All Army Activity 300/2010, August 2012b.

Headquarters, Department of the Army, *Army Command Policy*, Washington, D.C., Army Regulation 600-20, November 6, 2014.

Headquarters, Department of the Army, *Noncommissioned Officer Guide*, TC7-22.7 (Field Manual 7-22.7), April 15, 2015a. As of March 11, 2011: http://www.usar.army.mil/Portals/98/Users/105/41/1641/Noncommissioned_Officer_Guide_TC_7-22.7_(7_April_2015).pdf

Headquarters, Department of the Army, *Leader Development*, Washington, D.C., Field Manual 6-22, June 2015b.

Headquarters, Department of the Army, *Personnel Evaluation: Evaluating Reporting System*, Washington, D.C., Army Doctrine Reference Publication 623-3, November 4, 2015c.

Headquarters, Department of the Army, *Enlisted Promotions and Reductions*, Washington, D.C., Army Regulation 600-8-19, April 25, 2017.

Hosek, James, and Paco Martorell, *How Have Deployments During the War on Terrorism Affected Reenlistment?* Santa Monica, Calif.: RAND Corporation, MG-873-OSD, 2009. As of March 11, 2018: https://www.rand.org/pubs/monographs/MG873.html

Hosek, James R., and Michael G. Mattock, *Learning About Quality: How the Quality of Military Personnel Is Revealed over Time,* Santa Monica, Calif.: RAND Corporation, MR-1593-OSD, 2003. As of March 11, 2018: https://www.rand.org/pubs/monograph_reports/MR1593.html

HQDA—*See* Headquarters, Department of the Army.

Koedel, Cory, Kata Mihaly, and Jonah E. Rockoff, "Value-Added Modeling: A Review," *Economics of Education Review*, Vol. 47, August 2015, pp. 180–195.

Koh, William L., Richard M. Steers, and James R. Terborg, "The Effects of Transformational Leadership on Teacher Attitudes and Student Performance in Singapore," *Journal of Organizational Behavior*, Vol. 16, No. 4, 1995, pp. 319–333.

Laurence, Janice H., Jennifer Naughton, and Dickie A. Harris, "Attrition Revisited: Identifying the Problem and Its Solutions," Alexandria, Va.: U.S. Army Research Institute for the Behavioral and Social Sciences, Army Research Institute Research Note 96-20, January 1996.

Lyle, David S., and John Z. Smith, "The Effect of High-Performing Mentors on Junior Officer Promotion in the U.S. Army," *Journal of Labor Economics*, Vol. 32, No. 2, April 2014, pp. 229–258.

Maertz, Carl P., Rodger W. Griffeth, Nathanael S. Campbell, and David G. Allen, "The Effects of Perceived Organizational Support and Perceived Supervisor Support on Employee Turnover," *Journal of Organizational Behavior*, Vol. 28, No. 8, November 2007, pp. 1059–1075.

Noncommissioned Officer Education System, "U.S. Army Training and Doctrine Command, Institute for NCO Professional Development," April 25, 2016. As of April 8, 2018: http://www.tradoc.army.mil/INCOPD/index.html

Office of the Deputy Assistant Secretary of the Army for Cost and Economics, U.S. Army, "Cost Management: Resource Informed Decision Making and Performance Management—Framework, Methodology, Cost of Recruiting, and IMT—Case Study," briefing presentation provided to RAND, October 2015.

Office of the Under Secretary of Defense (Comptroller)/Chief Financial Officer, *Operation and Maintenance Overview Fiscal Year 2016 Budget Estimates*, February 2015.

Rich, Gregory A., "The Sales Manager as a Role Model: Effects on Trust, Job Satisfaction, and Performance of Salespeople," *Journal of the Academy of Marketing Science*, Vol. 25, No. 4, September 1997, pp. 319–328.

Rivkin, Steven G., Eric A. Hanushek, and John F. Kain, "Teachers, Schools, and Academic Achievement," *Econometrica*, Vol. 73, No. 2, February 2005, pp. 417–458.

Riley, Ryan P., Katelyn J. Cavanaugh, Jon J. Fallesen, and Rachell L. Jones, "2015 Center for Army Leadership Annual Survey of Army Leadership (CASAL): Military Leader Findings," Fort Leavenworth, Kan.: Center for Army Leadership, Technical Report 2016-01, July 2016. As of March 13, 2018:
https://usacac.army.mil/sites/default/files/documents/cal/2015CASALMilitaryLeaderFindingsReport.pdf

Riley, Ryan, Josh Hatfield, Tyler Freeman, Jon J. Fallesen, and Katie M. Gunther, *2013 Center for Army Leadership Annual Survey of Army Leadership (CASAL): Main Findings*, Fairfax, Va.: ICF International, Inc., Technical Report 2014-01, April 2014.

Smith, Brenda D., "Job Retention in Child Welfare: Effects of Perceived Organizational Support, Supervisor Support, and Intrinsic Job Value," *Children and Youth Services Review*, Vol. 27, No. 2, February 2005, pp. 153–169.

Tice, Jim, "New Rules for Enlisted Promotions," *Army Times*, February 23, 2015. As of March 15, 2018:
https://www.armytimes.com/news/your-army/2015/02/23/new-rules-for-enlisted-promotions/

U.S. Army Human Resources Command, "New NCOER Information Brief," January 6, 2015a. As of March 9, 2018:
http://www.ftmeade.army.mil/directorates/dhr/mpd/NCOER.pdf

U.S. Army Human Resources Command, "Senior Centralized Enlisted Army Promotion System," September 11, 2015b. As of September 18, 2015:
https://www.hrc.army.mil/TAGD/Senior%20Centralized%20Enlisted%20Army%20Promotion%20System

U.S. Department of Defense, "Military Compensation," website, undated. As of March 15, 2017:
http://militarypay.defense.gov

Ward, Michael P., and Hong W. Tan, *The Retention of High-Quality Personnel in the U.S. Armed Forces*, Santa Monica, Calif.: RAND Corporation, R-3117-MIL, 1985. As of April 25, 2018:
https://www.rand.org/pubs/reports/R3117.html

Warrior Leader Course (MOD) 600-WLC Program of Instruction, March 2006.

Warrior Leader Course Program of Instruction, July 2014.

Wenger, Jennie W., and Apriel K. Hodari, "Predictors of Attrition: Attitudes, Behaviors and Educational Characteristics," Alexandria, Va.: CNA, CRM D0010146.A2/Final, July 2004. As of March 9, 2018:
https://www.cna.org/CNA_files/PDF/D0010146.A2.pdf